EVERYDAY EXTRAORDINARY
ENCOUNTERING FETISHISM WITH MARX, FREUD AND LACAN

FIGURES OF THE UNCONSCIOUS 4

Everyday Extraordinary: Encountering Fetishism with Marx, Freud and Lacan

Edited by

Christopher M. Gemerchak

Leuven University Press
2004

Published with the Support of K.U.Leuven Commissie voor Publicaties

© 2004 Leuven University Press / Presses Universitaires de Louvain / Universitaire Pers Leuven
Blijde-Inkomststraat 5, B-3000 Leuven (Belgium)

ISBN 90 5867 408 8
D / 2004 / 1869 / 58
NUR: 777

Cover: Lejon Tits

CONTENTS

Preface

PREFACE

If the tradition of Western thought has succeeded in its mission, then in fact we should no longer be concerned with fetishism. It is now common knowledge that the history of Western thought has been characterized by the attempt to eliminate fetishism in all its forms. We want truth without illusion, history without myth; we expect the real to be reasonable and objects—natural, technical or sexual—to be transparent and manageable. Symbolism has become anachronistic. We have replaced the alchemic poetics of fetishism with the myth of things "as they really are," and this we call progress. Progress, however, is not a linear process. Misrecognition of reality is a constitutive element of advancing knowledge. History and the sciences, not unlike sexual development, move in fits and starts, and are punctuated with crises. These crises arise when belief in reality, of the world or of faith, is undermined, and what had appeared to be natural is not only discovered to be a representation, but a misrepresentation. That which defies our expectations of reality is frequently revealed to be the site of another truth. But if this is the course that knowledge must travel, then one must assume that we are habitually in error, that the ideas, truths, objects and actions to which we cling so as to secure some sense of certainty, some sense of our own identity in a mercilessly changing environment, are but vapours and mists that disguise the lack of any solid ground. This is disturbing to say the least. One cannot enjoy a normal life when every certainty is in doubt. Which gods will save us?

Fetishism used to be a question of gods. Momentary, material gods perhaps, but nonetheless powerful and wielding a sacred aura—at least within the closed, some would say perverse economy of purposive veneration. Now fetishism seems to be a question of the gods' disappearance, in more than one sense a crisis of faith. The fetish commemorates the crisis, marking the space of this disappearance. Fetishism is no longer seen as the immediate presence of an embodied force, but is rather a fetishism *de la chose perdu*, a nostalgia for lost essence and significant relations, and a displacement of this fetishized essence onto an object-screen. This has gradually led to a hollowing out of the fetish, such that today we find a loss of its materiality altogether, with the emphasis instead on the purely structural generation of objective illusion, an illusion that hides no reality except the effectiveness of the structure.

The vision of fetishism presented in this volume rotates on the axis of the disappearance or presence of something—the maternal phallus, the female body, the Lacanian *Chose*, an ontological ground—and investigates the attempt of the subject to come to terms with this absence or presence through the construction of a fetish. While our particular approaches, contexts and conclusions differ, the contributions converge in the attempt to determine the sense in which the fetish serves as a mediator in this process, and in so doing attempt to identify the generative causality and efficacy of the fetish, as well as the desires and anxieties from which it arises. To the extent that the fetish responds to a disappearance, we find that it does so in such a way that fixes or freezes time at the moment just prior to this disappearance, thereby performing the double gesture of disguising the loss and indicating the site of return. To the extent that the fetish responds to a presence, to a figure of alterity and difference frequently excessive and traumatic, we will examine the manner in which the fetish functions as a support to the subject's identity in the face of this threatening reality, seeing it function in one of its original senses as a form of protection to preserve a narcissistic universe.

However, if the question of fetishism were merely to be reduced to this structural opposition of *pars pro toto* or *pars pro nihilo*, this would not only situate fetishism within a classic metaphysical structure, where it does not in fact belong, but would dissipate a great portion of its evocative force, which springs precisely from its ambiguity—namely, its inability to be classified within the clear categories of representational thought and the logic of equivalence. If we were to take, for instance, the mature Freudian notion of the fetish as a substitute for the "absent" phallus of the mother, which will be the topic of much debate in the texts that follow, and situate it within the classic dynamic of presence and absence, then we would have to conclude that the absence of the phallus is an ontological modification of its presence. This clearly cannot be the case, insofar as there never was a presence for which the absence can serve as an alternative. Rather, its perceived absence relies on the infantile narcissistic expectation of, or primitive belief in, its presence, from which standpoint its absence is relegated to the realm of sheer possibility—a traumatic fiction perhaps, but nevertheless with real repercussions.

Similarly, if the fetish is seen as the site where a real material presence is embodied, or where an event involving contingent and capricious aspects comes to be crystallized, what are we to say is the relation of the fetish-object to its content? Is it sign, symbol or dissimulation? Does it function to preserve its content from oblivion, or to send it straight back? Does it serve to domesticate the heterogeneous elements contained within, to objectify them and submit them to thought and judgment, or does the fetish serve as a point of dazzling brilliance and nonconceptual significance? In four of the essays that follow (Moyaert, Goux, Nixon, De Block), we find these questions addressed specifically in relation to the figure of the female, the feminine, the woman, the mother. The woman remains the classic focal point of fetishistic interest, but the interpretations of the woman found in these essays, as well as the conclusions that are drawn, are anything but dated. The woman is the hinge of desire, the point where desire either gets trapped in an enclosed, perverse world of the Same, or enters into a symbolic life and a world of sexual difference and alterity.

In the introductory essay, "Fetishism, Desire and Finitude: The Artful Dodge," I attempt to bring our general approach and issues into focus through an analysis of the three traditional approaches to fetishism: the definition and critique of "primitive" fetishism; Marx's commodity fetishism and its role in the formation of the postmodern treatment of fetishism; and the psychoanalytic approach, with emphasis on Freud and Lacan. Acknowledging that fetishism neither belongs to a single culture or historical period, nor admits of conceptual unity, I nevertheless attempt to find some guiding thread that may be operative in all versions of fetishism. Ultimately identifying an expanded notion of Freudian disavowal as the possible glue to bind together the divergent theories, I posit fetishism as a reification of desire. Where desire endlessly explores reality for a satisfaction that is never forthcoming, the fetish steps in to close the circuit of desire by providing a partially satisfying solution, and does so in the attempt to protect the subject from the world's non-conformity to desire's highest expectations. Then, drawing a structural analogy between castration and finitude, I suggest that fetishism achieves the disavowal of the latter as much as the former.

Paul Moyaert, in his "Fetishism and the Vicissitudes of the Object in Sublimation According to Freud and Lacan," analyzes the distinction between the Freudian and Lacanian account of sublimation as based on their opposing views of what happens to the object of sublimation, and addresses their varying approaches to this object by means of their understanding of fetishism. He demonstrates the difference between Freud's and Lacan's notions of sublimation by determining whether or not the fetish has a perverse, centripetal function (Freud) or a sublimated, centrifugal function (Lacan). The key to the perverse or sublimated version of fetishism is the reaction of the subject to the Lacanian Thing, *la Chose*, which Moyaert illustrates with the scenario of courtly love: the anxious and rapturous love of the knight for an ambiguous figure of woman. In the perverse scenario, *la Chose* becomes an object, effectively narrowing and blocking the sexual instincts; in the sublimated scenario, the object suggests *la Chose*, resulting in an expansion and increased intensity of instinctual life.

Jean-Joseph Goux, in his "Vertigo of Substitutes: Fetish and Trophy," picks up the thread where Moyaert left off, charting the transformation of perverse desire into symbolic desire. But in Goux's case, he does so in the course of the attempt to find a myth that would correspond to fetishistic desire. Such a myth is conspicuously absent in Freud, as Goux argues that Freud's preferred myth, that of Oedipus, is inappropriate for illustrating fetishism. Rather, he finds a series of myths charting the passage of a male hero through incestuous desire and into symbolic exchange. Within the perspective of the confrontation with alterity and the fetishistic tendency to the reduction thereof, the central theme of this passage is the moment when the monstrous in women, or the monstrous incestuous desire for a woman, is conquered and marked by a sacred trophy-fetish. The trophy both serves as protection against the abysmal monster-mother and grants access to the non-maternal female. Whether the fetish can be conceived as a trophy becomes the central question in deciding the function of the fetish.

Andreas De Block, with his essay, "Genital Constructions: A Critique of Freud's "Fetishism"," revisits two of the themes previously encountered—the confrontation with a threatening aspect of woman and fetishism as an expansion of libidinal interests—but challenges the Freudian doctrine in which fetishism arises from castration anxiety and a "splitting" of the ego. Thus he takes a stand against any universal aetiology. Fetishism, in short, is not a genital construction. Rather, De Block, here siding with Goux, entertains the notion that fetishism might be based on an aversion to women, in particular their corporeality, and that it serves to protect the subject from losing his identity in undifferentiated embodiment by creating a distance between the subject and the female. Giving feminist discourse its say, he argues that the fetishist gesture so conceived amounts to an objectification of women and a reduction of their alterity and worth. Ultimately, he makes the case that it may not be anxiety at all that lies at the root of fetishistic sexuality, but rather boredom.

Mignon Nixon, in her essay, "What's so Funny about Fetishism?", also addresses the structural dynamic of the subject's ambiguous attitude of recognition and denial of a threatening reality—also the female body—but does so in order to turn the tables on the homogeneously masculine doctrine of fetishism and to move toward a reading that may account for feminine fetishism. With an unexpected move, rather than relying on the standard reproaches to Freud's reductive treatment of feminine sexuality, Nixon builds her case based on the fertile congruity of fetishism and humor. Where fetishism fails to enable the subject to transform its conflictual relation to reality, remaining fixed in a risible repetition of the same failed escapes, humor puts the conflict in an alternative perspective in such a way that allows the subject to come to terms with reality. Nixon then demonstrates her proposal by analyzing a selection of particularly fetishistic artworks by Louise Bourgeois. The works she has chosen represent various phases in Bourgeois' relation to the artistic depiction of the female fetish: from caricaturizing the masculine doctrine of female *as* fetish, to the depiction of what a fetish *for* the female might be, and finally to an ironic convergence of fetishism and the feminine in which the artist recognizes the woman's participation in the male perversion, but transforms and neutralizes its degrading aspects by means of humor.

The final essay, Egidius Berns' "Fetishes and Ghosts: Marx and Derrida," departs from the psychoanalytic terrain to treat of Marx's notion of fetishism and the more recent interpretations and critiques thereof, Jacque Derrida's in particular. Focusing on the preponderance of ghostly images and metaphors in Marx, Berns charts the development of the ghost until it issues in Derrida's "hauntology." He begins with an analysis of Marx's fetishism, explaining how the fetish is to be seen as a ghost, and why Marx tries to exorcise this phantom. The reason for Marx's efforts at exorcism, however, reveals an ontological presupposition lurking behind the scenes. And this, of course, is what draws Derrida's attention. Berns explains how Derrida, through his reading of Marx, comes to identify fetishism with ontology, and how this identification does not extend to the ghost. The ghostly, rather, will serve to call ontology into question. Ultimately, Berns considers whether or not Derrida falls into the same trap as Marx—despite being lured with bait of an entirely different scent—and gives an indication as to Derrida's way out of this pitfall.

This volume of collected essays is the fourth book in the series, *Figures of the Unconscious*, and continues where its predecessors left off, joining the forces of philosophy and psychoanalysis to attend to the the human province at its most vulnerable points of affliction, of confusion, error and uncertainty. Fetishism is located at just such a point, the point where the open wound of the spirit is touched by the world, and serves as a salve to cover this wound. But as we continue, we will find that fetishism is not solely a means to hide our deficiencies and cover our losses. It is not merely a passive response to a world that does not meet our expectations, but may provide structure and depth to subjective life. A poem or song, for instance, might attempt to give expression to a feeling of infinite mourning, but its words are not equal to the experience. Are we then to condemn the imitation because it fails to accurately represent what is felt in the flood of immediacy? Similarly, are we to castigate fetishism for its deficiencies while ignoring its attempts to repair the fractured soul, to give shape to formless desire and rhythm to the atonal drone of anxiety? Who will be the judge of this conflictual figure of the unconscious? No judgment will be handed down in this collection of essays. We will simply argue in the attempt to create a convincing case.

*

* *

Publication of this book was made possible by funding provided by the Fonds voor Wetenschappelijke Onderzoek—Vlaanderen.

*

Considering the frequent citation of *The Standard Edition of the Complete Psychological Works of Sigmund Freud*, ed. and trans. James Stratchey (London: Hogarth Press, 1953-62), all references to Freud's *Standard Edition* will be indicated by *SE* followed by the volume and the page number.

*

The editor would like to thank the following individuals for their generous and invaluable assistance: Drew Dalton, Michael Deckard, Heidi Klein, Cal Ledsham and Reneé Ryan.

Paul Moyaert's "Fetishism and the Vicissitudes of the Object in Sublimation According to Freud and Lacan"; Andreas De Block's "Genital Constructions: A Critique of Freud's "Fetishism" "; and Egidius Bern's "Fetishes and Ghosts: Marx and Derrida," were translated from their original Dutch by the editor. Any loss of subtlety or eloquence is entirely his fault.

Christopher Gemerchak

FETISHISM, DESIRE AND FINITUDE:
THE ARTFUL DODGE

Christopher Gemerchak

There is a peculiar, even defining difficulty one faces when attempting to grasp the notion of fetishism. It is a problem not unlike when dealing with a liquid substance. One cannot seize it without condensing it into an immobile form, without crystallizing it, thereby removing its most essential characteristic as a liquid. All one can do is contain it, place it in a context, which allows one to control and use it. This, however, will neither prevent evaporation, the dissipation of its substance into thin air, nor its subsequent recondensation, its return to substance in some other location, in some other form. At the heart of liquid substance is an emptiness which precipitates its incessant transformation. Likewise at the heart of fetishism, both on the side of the fetish object and the fetishistic subject, there is an internal contradiction between brute materiality and evanescent dissimulation, essence and appearance, which makes it flow.

And flow it does, effortlessly seeping into the terminology of psycho-analysis as a peculiar libidinal organization that divides the subject against itself; into anthropology as one of the core elements of primitive religions; into Marxism as the peculiar objective form (the commodity) taken by socio-economic relations; and into popular culture and language as a general term for a curiously strong interest in an idea, a practice, a thing or a person. Being everywhere and yet nowhere in particular, the problem of fetishism, in short, is to know precisely what one is speaking about when one speaks of it.

Now, this may indeed seem curious, for judging by the regularity and nonchalant certainty with which the word "fetish" and its derivatives—"fetishism" and "fetishistic"—are used in a wide variety of contexts, its meaning seems evident enough. A fetish is an object or idea that, *for no apparent reason*, receives an excessive amount of attention if not devotion: one has a chocolate fetish, a leather fetish, a fetish for exercise or conspiracy theories, a fetish for pronounced clavicles, for nurses, for nurses with pronounced clavicles, or one may polish one's car with a decidedly fetishistic urgency. Given this degree of generality, the scope of fetishism would seem so broad that one should rather ask who is *not* a fetishist. My primary goal here will not be to specify what would be deserving of the label of fetishism, but to attempt to unmask an invariable genealogy behind it.

The first task then seems simply to try to locate the phenomenon in question, to find some unifying principle, although it is precisely against such an attempt that we are often warned. As Marcel Mauss famously remarked, "the notion of the fetish should ... definitively disappear from science,"

13

precisely because it "corresponds to nothing definite."[1] Jean Pouillon reinforces this assessment: "It would be vain to pretend to give a general definition which would subsume the diverse senses of fetishism."[2] Despite this implicit advice, we will decline to be deterred in our pursuit of some unitary approach to fetishism, and to provide some clarification regarding the impulse behind it.

Let us then start with a classic approach and claim that the "invariant predicate"[3] of the fetish is that it is a substitute for something else, an *Ersatz* for a more primordial instance of reality that is, at least temporarily, missing. One's girlfriend is studying abroad for a semester, but one keeps her shoes by the bed as a method to retain a semblance of her presence and mediate one's loneliness; one's God has not made an appearance recently, and one needs some help or reassurance, so one holds fast to one's crucifix or amulet and raises one's eyes to the heavens. In short, there is a referential structure in which a material sign makes something present in its absence. Are these examples worthy of the accusation of fetishism? Can fetishism be circumscribed within this oppositional epistemology of a real thing and its derivative representative, signified and signifier, non-substitute and substitute, essence and accident? If so, then we are working with a quite weak and indistinct notion of fetishism, one that would hardly be deserving of what Michel Leiris calls "le fétichisme qui ... reste à la base de notre existence humaine,"[4] and one which Derrida (following Freud and even Marx) deems inadequate to account for the phantom presences called fetishes.

Without abandoning this semiotic and substitutive model, however, let us consider two variations to its premise. We will first consider whether or not the *intensity* of the subject's attachment to the *Ersatz*-fetish could be the deciding factor in distinguishing fetishism from mere representation. An excessively intense attachment to an object that is essentially a sign for something else one values implies a degree of fixation on the materiality of the sign. This fixation effectively blocks the sign's referential function and implies some confusion regarding the object of attachment. In this case, fetishism would seem to be a result of subjective distortion, perhaps intellectual failure. Second, we will consider whether or not the *opacity* of the signifier obscures the ability of the subject to see through the *Ersatz*-fetish and recognize the original behind it. If this is the case, then it appears that fetishism may be based on an objective distortion to which any subject would unwittingly fall prey.

[1] Marcel Mauss, *Oeuvres II* (Paris: Éditions de Minuit, 1969), 244.

[2] Jean Pouillon, "Fétiches sans fétichisme," in *Objets du fétichisme*, (Paris: Nouvelle Revue de Psychanalyse, Numéro 2, automne 1970), 143.

[3] Jacques Derrida, *Glas*, trans. John P. Leavey, Jr. and Richard Randl (Lincoln: University of Nebraska Press, 1986), 209.

[4] "the fetishism which ... remains at the base of our human existence." Michel Leiris, "Alberto Giacometti," *Documents* vol. 1, no. 4 (1929), 209.

In order to illustrate these two variations of substitution, we will refer to two relatively recent films whose popularity is such that few will be able to claim not to have seen them, namely, *Pulp Fiction* and *The Matrix*. In both of these films, one finds an accurate illustration of *Ersatz* fetishism, though they are manifest in radically different guises. Despite this divergence, however, we will discover in both what may—although still in a classic sense—be delimited as the core structure behind fetishism proper: the *Ersatz* ceases to be an *Ersatz* and is taken to be the thing itself. The substitute may still refer to something else, but this referral is hidden. Formulated in broader terms, in every case of fetishism an "error of attribution"[5] occurs such that a thing is invested with a status it does not actually have, effectively closing the gap between the object and that to which it should refer. This 'error' occurs in such a variety of ways, however, that this definition cannot provide any real specificity regarding fetishism as such. Our investigation must therefore address how and why this error occurs, what the underlying structure of this fetishistic error could be, and what it tells us about the subject or group that comes under its sway? As announced in the title of this essay, I believe fetishism reveals something fundamental about human desire and arises from a particular relation of the subject to its own finitude, its own particularity as an individual. Yet with a decidedly fetishistic ambiguity, it may reveal something about the subject, desire and finitude, only to deny and conceal it. This will become clearer as we continue.

In the first film (*Pulp Fiction*, 1994, U.S.A.) there is an example of what may be called "primitive" fetishism, one which makes clear that the primitive in us is not just a distant memory, is in fact contemporary. Once we have seen an example of the contemporary primitive, I will sketch the origin of this understanding of fetishism and examine the reasons for the condemnation it received in the period leading up to the Enlightenment, whereupon "fetishism" became a universally accepted denunciation of irrational practices. The second film (*The Matrix*, 1999, U.S.A.) depicts what one may call an ideological reading of fetishism as inaugurated by Marx, which continues to inform the structuralist and semiological approaches to this issue.

Now, given the fact that the term "fetishism" may justifiably be used to describe the two radically divergent scenarios depicted in these films, one of the following conclusions must be drawn: either "fetishism" is nothing but a shifting metaphor to be indiscriminately applied as one sees fit, or there is in fact a common core lurking beneath the appearance of diversity. Is there some

---

[5] J. Pouillon, "Fétiches sans fétichisme," *op. cit.*, 135. Pouillon states, "In every case, the error of the fetishist is an error of attribution, but for Marx, it consists in attributing a status of a thing to that which is not one, while inversely, for Comte and for Hegel, it consists in attributing a status of being animated to that which is not, while for Freud it is to place a reality there where there is none." This summary is only roughly accurate, yet gives a sense of the problem of generalizing fetishism.

unitary structure and function of the fetish? Is there some common motivation for its appearance? To investigate these questions I will discuss Freud's earlier treatments of fetishism (1905 and 1909) and Marx's notion of commodity fetishism. Ultimately, however, Freud's final approach to fetishism as found in his article "Fetishism" (1927), and the notion of disavowal (*Verleugnung*) proposed therein will serve as our guide. The notion of disavowal provides a structure serviceable for the various phenomena that belong under the label of "fetishism." And, as we will see, it is this structure that Lacan and Mannoni assumed in their respective treatments of this issue. However, only by expanding Freud's notion of disavowal will we be able to understand fetishism as a fundamental possibility for the human subject.

1. Pulp Fiction *and Charles de Brosses*

One of the storylines running through *Pulp Fiction* concerns a boxer and his wristwatch. This wristwatch, to use the terminology with which Freud described the elusive maternal penis in his definitive article on fetishism, is "no ordinary" watch, but is rather a "particular and quite special" watch, one for which the boxer is willing to risk his life rather than face its loss. It is indeed astonishing to consider that the boxer's excessive valuation of the watch has nothing to do with any intrinsic qualities of the watch itself. This particular time-measuring device is not in the least extraordinary, has no exceptional physical qualities, nor is it particularly beautiful. How then does it acquire its excessive value for the boxer? The evident answer: by being a material object that mediates the relation of the subject to a wider symbolic network, namely, his dead ancestors. That is, the history of the watch endows it with a symbolic value for the subject and makes it unique, irreplaceable, an-economic. This history was told to the boxer, when he was still a young boy, by a veteran of the Vietnam War who had suffered harsh imprisonment along with the boxer's father.

The veteran visits the boy with the intention of bequeathing him the watch. Holding the battered watch aloft in his hand, not altogether unlike a priest consecrating the host, the veteran tells the boy how the watch had passed from generation to generation in his family, eventually becoming his father's. He tells him of the great pains his father endured to be able to pass the watch on to the boy, how the boy's father had to hide the watch in his anus for five years of imprisonment to prevent his captors from confiscating it. His father does not return alive to give the boy his watch but he had sealed a pact with his fellow soldier (who in turn hid the watch in his own anus for two more years) to ensure that the boy would receive it. The boy assumes the pact when he receives the watch and he continues the tradition of safeguarding it at all costs so he can in turn pass it on to his own son. The extremes to which he is willing to go in order to do so, while arguably not matching those of his father,

16

baffle his girlfriend who is unaware of the exceptional significance of the otherwise unremarkable, "silly" old watch, and who finds his intense attachment to it not only incomprehensible, but absurd.

Where are we to locate the fetishism in this story? The answer seems obvious enough: it is the boxer's intense attachment to his fetish, the watch. But is this necessarily the case? Is an excessively strong valuation of a material object necessarily fetishism? Or might not the girlfriend's incredulity at the boxer's attachment to the watch in fact be the source of fetishism here? In analyzing these questions, we should be able to gain an accurate picture of the concept and development of primitive fetishism. Before we arrive at this analysis, however, it may be useful to address what may be called its pre-history, as the phenomenon first called "fétichisme" by President Charles de Brosses in his *Du culte des dieux fétiches* (1760) had been known and documented long before receiving this title.[6] I will analyze just a few select points from this pre-history that have been retained in almost every version of fetishism.[7]

The first point is a concern with deception, a concern implied in the very root of the word "fetish." As William Pietz explains, the term can be traced back to Roman mercantile society where it receives multiple significations. The word fetish derives from the Latin *facticius* or *factitius*, adjectives formed from the verb *facere* ("to make"), and simply mean a fabricated, man-made object as opposed to products emerging from natural processes (Pietz 13, 24-5). In another usage of the same terms, however, not only the method of production is at issue; rather, emphasis is placed on the "virtue" of the goods produced, which derives from the means of production. Artificial production yields objects of inferior appearance and this influences the judgment of the quality of what is made. However, a highly artistic manufacturer who, much like an illusionist, succeeds in creating a highly attractive and believable

---

[6] Charles de Brosses, *Du Culte des Dieux Fétiches, ou Parallèle de l'ancienne Religion de l'Egypte avec la Religion actuelle de Nigritie* (France: Fayard, Corpus des Oeuvres de Philosophie en Langue Française, 1988). The most thorough treatment of the history and development of fetishism and the fetish is found in a series of articles written by William Pietz, entitled "The Problem of the Fetish" in the journal *Res* (9, Autumn 1987; 13, Spring 1987; 16, Autumn 1988). Further reference to these articles will be indicated by (Pietz), followed by the issue number and page number.

[7] Central to this pre-history is the conflict over religious images, symbols, and practices. The concern with fetishism in early Christianity develops in the context of rooting out deviant variations of Christian themes: witchcraft, idolatry and superstition are rogue versions of the Christian concepts of creation, incarnation, and salvation. Religious criticisms directed at the Africans from the Portuguese Catholics, and then at the Portuguese Catholics from the Dutch Protestants, as well as the debates within the Christian Church itself, form an integral part of the debate over fetishism. These issues will not, however, directly enter into my discussion.

product despite its inferior substantial reality can effectively deceive the buyer and dupe him into paying more than the real value of the object.

That is, an object can be so fabricated as to give the impression that it is of superior value in comparison to a natural product, but this is a mere appearance veiling its unworthiness, an artificial shine more seductive than the unpolished original, yet a shine that is as empty as it is promising. Such is the third and final meaning of *facticius* as found in Pliny's *Natural History*. Speaking of a "flower of salt" found on the banks of the river Nile, Pliny says, "It is adulterated too and colored by red ochre, or usually by ground crockery; this sham is detected by water, which washes out the artificial [*facticium*] color, while the genuine is only removed by oil...".[8] As Pietz points out:

> Here *facticium* means "artificial" in the sense of "materially altered by human effort in order to deceive"... . The morally neutral opposition between "man-made" and "naturally produced" now becomes a valuative contrast between "natural" (in the sense of "authentic," "true") and "artificial" (in the sense of "unnatural," and "deliberately false"), (Pietz 13, 25).

Deception, then, is related to metaphysical concerns, perhaps even anxiety, regarding essence and appearance, truth and falsehood. And so is the fetish.

Issuing directly from this first distinction between true essence and deceitful appearance, the second invariable aspect of fetishism found in this pre-history involves a conflict over who has access to the truth and who is living in falsehood. The real beginning of fetishism proper is located in the classic dynamic of the same and the other. Charles de Brosses, for instance, claims that fetishism has existed everywhere and always as the initial, infantile stage of religion, albeit "with the exception of *the chosen race*": the white, European Christians who never sank to such folly.[9] Fetishism thus begins with the belief that one has privileged access to the truth, while the other—the fetishist—makes an error of attribution and takes the false appearance or accidental object to be the thing itself. In its original sense, fetishism is less a term of description than it is an accusation, principally about the absurdity of someone else's actions. Fetishism, in short, is always *somebody else's problem*: having a fetish is not a problem for the fetishist, but for the observer; the observer has clarity of consciousness, the other is the fetishist.[10] This is

---

[8] Pliny, *Natual History*, B. 31, section 42. Citation from Pietz 13, 25.

[9] "A l'exception de la race choisie, il n'y a aucune Nation qui n'ait été dans cet état [de purs sauvages plongés dans l'ignorance et dans la barbarie]." C. de Brosses, *Du culte des dieux fétiches, op.cit.*, 13.

[10] As Freud points out, a fetish "is seldom felt by [its adherents] as the symptom of an ailment accompanied by suffering. Usually they are quite satisfied with it..." Sigmund Freud, "Fetishism" *SE XXI*, 147. See as well the commentary by Bruno Latour in his *Petite réflexion sur le culte moderne des dieux faitiches* (Le Plessis-Robinson: Synthélabo (Collection: Les Empêcheurs de penser en rond), 1996):

why "the discourse of the fetish has always been a critical discourse about the false objective values of a culture from which the observer is personally distanced."[11]

In this regard, we find that fetishism develops in the confrontation between secular Europeans and the Other, the heterogeneous, (in this case) alien culture and its consciousness. The origin of fetishism is located in the struggle between European enlightenment and African darkness as two distinct forms of consciousness: one independent from nature and—if we are naïve enough to believe what people say about themselves—free from superstition; the other radically confused and nature-dependent, "ignorant and fearful" as de Brosses often repeats. The initial manifestation of this conflict is found in the disparity between the rational economic principles of the European merchants who traveled to West Africa in the sixteenth and seventeenth centuries, and the frustrating, religion-clouded socio-economic practices of the natives with whom they entered into relations of trade.[12] As Pietz tells us, "the idea of the fetish originated in a mercantile intercultural space by the ongoing trade relations between cultures so radically different as to be mutually incomprehensible" (Pietz 13, 24). And, as we are currently seeing in the increasingly violent cultural conflicts, when a culture that considers its *own particular* history and thought to be *universal* history and thought confronts cultural practices that appear alien, it does not hesitate to deem them absurd.

However, while the Europeans condemned them as absurd, they did not hesitate to have dealings with this irrational peoples, for transactions with these sort of people could be extremely profitable to those *lacking personal attachment* to the items they were trading. This attachment, engendering a bizarre overvaluation, was in fact the core of the disparity between economic principles that made trading at once so frustrating and profitable for the Europeans. On the one hand, the West Africans appeared to the Europeans to be suffering from a fundamental confusion regarding the nature of material objects, *feitiços* or *fetissos* as the Portuguese called them, insofar as they saw these objects as permeated with religious values and quasi-personalized natural forces, thereby distorting their 'real' commercial value. On the other hand, and for the 'wrong' reasons—that is, non-economic, religious, or personal and thus arbitrary reasons—they would overvalue things that the Europeans considered "trifles" or "trash"[13] and practically give away what

---

[11] "Comment définir un anti-fétichiste? C'est celui qui accuse un *autre* d'être fétichiste," 24, author's emphasis.
Pietz 9, 14. See as well Alfonzo M. Iacono, *Le Fétichisme, Histoire d'un concept* (Paris: Presses Universitaires de France, 1992), where he pays particular attention to the viewpoint from which the observer has access to the observed.

[12] The analysis that follows is principally based on Pietz 13 and 16.

[13] "A Lion's Tail ... a Bird's Feather ... a Pebble, a Bit of Rag, a Dog's Leg; or, in short, any thing they fancy." From the travelogue of William Smith, *A Voyage to New Guinea*, cited in Pietz, Res 13, 41.

19

was truly of value, namely gold. This 'false' estimation of the value of things—which Marx reveals as being the fundamental confusion determining the form of consciousness within the capitalist system, thereby exposing the primitive inheritance of advanced market exchange—naturally led to inordinate profits for the European traders. If the natives suffered economically, it was for having failed to reap the rewards of embracing dispassionate Enlightenment rationality, or alternatively, for having an overly intense relation to their objects.

Their double or even triple error of attribution, each of which testified to a distorted, superstitious, and false sense of causality, led them not only to be ridiculed, but plundered. Symptomatic of the pre-enlightened mind, primitive fetishists attributed a variety of purposeful intentionalities to the mechanistic natural world, and believed that if they could divine those purposes they could *reverse their lack of control* over nature and *make it conform to their own desires*. Thus, on the one hand, they saw personal forces operating where—according to the Europeans—only natural, objective forces should have been perceived. On the other hand, they believed these personified forces to be embodied in certain material objects, effectively enabling them to wear the god around their neck or carry it in a sack. But most frustratingly, as mentioned above, they saw divine or religious forces animating objects in which only the social forces of material production should have been evident.

With regard to the nature of the confusion apparently suffered by the Africans, one finds that the only initial agreement among ethnologists and anthropologists with respect to fetishism was the simple fact of confusion itself. The earliest theorists of primitive peoples made the assumption that the primitives, being unduly under the sway of immediate concrete reality, had a fundamental incapacity for abstract thought, living rather in a state of "perpetual infancy."[14] This incapacity rested on a tendency to condensation, the gluing of content and container characteristic of mythical thought and language.[15] Put another way using a Heideggerian neologism, primitive thought does not issue from the dualism of an autonomous subject facing a distinct object but rather from a subject that is always already "conditioned" or

---

[14] Cf. de Brosses, 13, *et. al.*

[15] "For language there is at first no sharp dividing line between the word and its signification, between the content of the representation and the content of the mere sign... . The nominalistic view, in which words are mere conventional signs ... is a product of late reflection..." Ernst Cassirer, *The Philosophy of Symbolic Forms: Vol.2, Mythical Thought,* trans. Ralph Manheim (New Haven: Yale University Press, 1955), 25. Cassirer is notably not of the view proclaiming the lack of abstract thinking among the primitives (mythical consciousness). Rather, he sees mythical thought as a first step toward spiritual abstraction, and while on the one hand it remains bound to its material signs (fetishes), it also starts to rise above them.

"be-thinged" [*bedingt*] by the world.[16] Consequently, primitive peoples seemed unable to categorize their objects into different spheres, but rather condensed the practical, religious, social, aesthetic, economic, and the magical into a single object. Furthermore, they were judged to lack the facility to distinguish between a sensible substrate and that which imbues it with meaning.

This perspective is the point of departure for the modern history of the concept of fetishism. Charles de Brosses, as mentioned above, coined the term "fétichisme" to describe the earliest form of religion, a "purile," "direct" cult dedicated to the worship of terrestrial things, "the first object that struck their fancy."[17] In keeping with the ideology of progress, de Brosses supposed that cultural and religious developments follow a natural course from blind, concrete immediacy to abstraction, with fetishism representing a "crude and primordial stage of humanity ... in which there was no capacity to distinguish the thing and its representation."[18] Lower on the scale than idolatry—which while unreasonable nevertheless refers beyond the immediate object— fetishism as a practice represented the "zero degree of the human faculty of representation and symbolization ... the direct divinization of objects."[19] Stuck in an infantile state and essentially swallowed by immediate concrete reality, the primitive is said to be incapable of making a distinction between a thing and that which it represents. It is only the more sophisticated Christians who are capable of this, as ambiguously demonstrated in the ceremony of the Catholic Eucharist, where the presence of God is affirmed in the host, which is venerated accordingly, but without taking the host for God. Indeed, one of the first mistakes of the original theory of fetishism is the naïve belief in naïve belief, which is why fetishism is said to have been nothing but an "immense misunderstanding" between cultures.[20]

[16] See in particular Heidegger's essay "The Thing" (*Das Ding*) in *Poetry, Language, Thought*, trans. A. Hofstadter (New York: Harper and Row, 1971), 167-179. Here one finds Heidegger's famous analysis of the jug as a thing that is not strictly produced by the hand of any subject, and effectively escapes the grasp of the subject by hiding itself in its very disclosure. Two points: the apparently determinate object is in fact no object at all, but a place of gathering for what dwells within its emptiness; the apparently constructive subject has shaped something that escapes its control. I believe these two points are essential when considering fetishism.

[17] C. de Brosses, 16.

[18] Iacono, *Fétichisme: Histoire d'un concept*, 53, *op. cit.*

[19] Ibid., 53-4

[20] M. Mauss, *Oeuvres II, op. cit.*, 245. Fetishism, as Mauss claims, "only corresponds to an immense misunderstanding between two civilizations, African and European; it has no other foundation than blind obedience to colonial usage..." See as well Latour in his *Petite réflexion*, "If they accuse the savages of fetishism, the Whites are nevertheless not naïve anti-fetishists. Belief will fall between Charybis and Scylla. We will have saved the Blacks from belief—now having become an accusation carried by the Whites on something that they do not

From an external point of view, the choice of some lowly profane object—"the first stone they come across,"[21] a tree, a dried monkey head—as an object of reverence does seem to be an arbitrary, capricious choice, an irrationally intense subjective attachment. Is this the case with the boxer's watch? Is the boxer's intense relation to the watch to be called fetishism with any accuracy? Now, I believe it is safe to say that, had Charles de Brosses seen *Pulp Fiction*, he would have certainly concluded that the boxer was a fetishist of the most primitive order, worshipping the watch as a god. And if we analyze the story from *Pulp Fiction*, we find that the boxer's girlfriend is in the same structural position as the ethnographers who observed African religious practices: she is mystified as to why the boxer's watch is of such importance because she is not aware that the watch bound him to his absent father, his father's father, etc., and that the watch is thus a material embodiment of his place in a symbolic order. She mistakenly perceives him to be engaged in an absurdity as extreme as directly divinizing the watch with no transcendent reference.

But if it does indeed have a referential structure, then the watch is not a fetish, but is merely a symbol. Taken in the strict sense, *a fetish*, insofar as it collapses the distinction between the referential thing and the Thing (the original object) to which it is held to refer, *does not refer beyond itself*. It cancels, in effect, its symbolic value. The watch on the other hand is a symbol in the sense that it both points beyond itself to the absent father/Thing, yet at the same time immediately embodies him in its material substance: the father is present in the watch, and so the watch cannot be replaced with a duplicate; but it would be naïve to say that the boxer mistakes his watch for his father. In a similar way, it is naïve to think that the "primitive" fetish object is either necessarily arbitrary, or that it is confused with what it embodies.

The boxer should allow us to refute de Brosses' claim for "zero symbolization" as it would seem that that the error of attribution that is here defining the fetish is not an error on the part of the fetishist at all. Rather, the error lay with the observer. In the eyes of de Brosses or the boxer's girlfriend, the boxer's attachment to the material object seems irrational and leaves them incredulous, though for slightly different reasons. The girlfriend is (at first) simply unaware of the heterogeneous significations condensed in the watch, and so misunderstands the boxer's attachment. Once this condensation is unraveled his attachment at least makes more sense. De Brosses, on the other hand, might even know that the watch is an earthly sign of a transcendent divinity (the father), but would conclude, because of his intense attachment to the material thing, that the boxer cannot tell them apart. This sort of

understand—but we will plunge the Whites into an abyss of naïveté. They believe that the others believe!", *op. cit.*, 24.

21 Georg Wilhelm Freidrich Hegel, *Philosophy of Mind*, trans. A.V. Miller (Oxford: Clarendon Press, 1971), 42. It should be noted that Hegel draws close to the theory of De Brosses here, insofar as both are bothered by the arbitrary—or for Hegel, purely subjective—character of fetishism.

attachment simply does not fit into his accepted scheme of signs, objects and value, principally insofar as the notion of a rational subject being determined by the objective world severely compromised the sense of autonomy that was blossoming in Europe at the time.

In this first instance then, it appears that fetishism is an observer's *misunderstanding of someone else's attachment* to an object. And it is this misunderstanding, rather than the intense attachment to the thing, that strips the object of its symbolic value. It thus seems that we have found at least an initial answer to our opening questions: fetishism is not simply an intense, immediate relation to an object or a subjective error of attribution; there is an intermingling of an intense attachment to an object with a degree of mystification regarding its referential structure. There are, however, degrees of blindness.

As suggested with the boxer, his overvaluation of the watch does not rely on what de Brosses believed to be a pure primitive blindness to the symbolic structure of his attachment. Neither, however, is this situation of total clarity. Keeping this admixture of knowledge and non-knowledge in mind, I would like to ask whether the intensity of the boxer's attachment to his watch betrays something more general and fundamental about his subjectivity. Might another sense of fetishism be thereby deduced? To answer this question it is important to understand that not all examples of significant objectivity arise from the direct referential structure we have been examining. It is often the case that *what* acquires significance for the fetishistic subject is in itself utterly insignificant. The salient point is only the fact of significance itself, the *intensity* with which something is experienced and believed.

Now, if we cannot say that the fetishization of an object rests on an awareness of what the object refers to or substitutes for, nor even—as with unenlightened peoples—on the mistaken reference to a god or force that does not exist, then one of two options are open to us: either we once again reduce fetishism to nothing but a dumb fascination for the concrete, which we have already ruled out as a misunderstanding; alternatively, the fetish is an embodiment of something real that nevertheless entirely escapes the subject. This has significant consequences.

I once again turn to our little story of the boxer and his watch: we know the watch is a type of representation (*Vorstellung*) of his dead father; we know it is overvalued and irreplaceable insofar as it somehow embodies and reveals his connection with his father, in a way rendering his absent father still present. But if my suggestion that the real motivation for the boxer's attachment to his watch cannot be directly derived from its referential structure, then the *Vorstellung* is in fact a *Verstellung*, a dissemblance, a disguise, a sham.[22] The more obvious aspect of the fetish as veiling its origin

---

[22]   *Verstellen* has many of the same connotations as fetish: to put one thing in place of another, substitute, shift, remove or displace, but also counterfeit and sham.

will be seen in greater detail in the section that follows on Marx. However, a more obscure and recalcitrant aspect of the fetish emerges when a redoubling of the dissimulation occurs, and the *Verstellung* (dissimulation) is taken for a *Vorstellung* (representation), exacerbating the distance between what one thinks one wants to retain, and the container in which one thinks one is housing it. As we see in the current example, the absence for which the fetish is a substitute is believed to have been made present in the substitute, but this is not at all the case, for the substitute derives from an entirely different absence. Nevertheless, the fetishistic subject will hold fast to it, for the fetish provides some degree of satisfaction, appeasing the desire to maintain or hedging against the anxiety of losing the boxer's link to his dead father.

But satisfaction rarely provokes extreme degrees of intensity. Intensity, rather, is more bound to the anxiety that what one has is not fully in one's possession, that it is withdrawing, always on the verge of being lost, that desire is not satisfied. Thus, the intensity of the fetishistic attachment might betray that the boxer is not going to extremes to protect the watch simply because it is his dead father's watch. Something else is at stake. Yet what *is* at stake is being occluded precisely by his attachment to the watch. The watch, in effect, *obstructs* the boxer's desire, *preventing* it from seeking to alleviate a sense of loss which is perhaps more primordial than the loss of his father. It provides a partially satisfying solution by effectively reifying desire, silencing the anxiety that comes from not knowing what it is that is guiding one's desire, and thus from the potential groundlessness of one's attachments. In short, the fetish-watch is the reification of desire. By proposing itself as a partially satisfactory object, one that is in the subject's possession and thus allows him or her to feel in control of an otherwise precarious situation, the watch effectively protects the subject from desire's infinite restlessness. And even further, perhaps by even intimating that it refers to something beyond itself, the real illusion of fetishism is established: the illusion that there is indeed something behind the fetish, for which the fetish serves as a veil. As we continue, I will try to clarify and unpack these cryptic speculations.

2. *Marx and* The Matrix

At first sight, an entirely different notion of fetishism than the one we have seen in *Pulp Fiction* is illustrated in the film, *The Matrix*. In contrast to fetishism as revealing the primitive tendency to fixate on a particular concrete object, this film depicts a postmodern vision of fetishism in an advanced capitalist society, the institutionalized structuring of social consciousness so as to create social reality as a comprehensive system of objective illusion—the

My attention was brought to this etymological play by Mark C. Taylor in his *Altarity* (Chicago: The University of Chicago Press, 1987), 45 n. 17.

fixation on empty signs rather than material substance.[23] Yet in the transition from the primitive to the postmodern, the ambivalence of truth and fiction, reality and belief are carried over, albeit in an alternative form.

The background of the film is as follows: artificial intelligence has finally become a reality, and once they got a few ideas in their heads intelligent machines revolted against the humans; a war ensued, and the machines have won, leaving the earth devastated and the sun shrouded by a nuclear winter; the machines now control the earth, and harvest the enslaved humans as their power supply; the humans are kept alive, though apparently asleep, in uterine tubs filled with an artificial anmniotic fluid. Now the interesting bit: the machines decide that if they want to keep the humans happy and submissive— although given their situation, it is unclear how they could be otherwise—they must be kept blind. To achieve this end, the machines develop the matrix, a computer-generated world plugged directly into the neural system of the comatose humans. This illusory world, however, is an exact replica of the world in which they were living prior to the war, so no one is aware that anything has changed. Like prototypical Althusserian subjects, they see the imaginary, ideological world the matrix-system wants them to see, and believe that the fabricated reality fed into their brains corresponds to their real conditions of existence, the Real to which they in fact have no access. Thus, while immersed in their biotechnical wombs, the humans nevertheless believe they are still living life just as it was before the war. The illusion is misleading precisely because it looks and feels *completely natural*, as just "the way things are." Their reality is fiction.

There is, however, a small group of humans who have evaded capture by the machines and live in the disenchanted, real world, "the desert of the real." In order to save the world (from technology, apparently), they need to find their savior (Neo) and free him from the matrix, the computer-generated illusory reality. In order to free him, it is not enough that he be removed from his state of submission to the system. Not only must he be enlightened as to the reality behind the illusion so he can recognize the real conditions of his existence, he must as well choose to renounce his belief in the illusion. The

---

[23]   Jean Baudrillard emphasizes the same point as Pietz in his essay, "Fetishism and Ideology: The Semiological Reduction," where he returns to the original sense of "fetish" as "artificial," "to imitate by signs," or "faking," (he notes that the Portuguese *feitiço* and the Spanish *afeitar*, "to paint, to adorn, to embellish" and *hechar*, "to do, to make" (whence *hechizo*: "artificial, feigned, dummy") have the same root in the Latin *facticius*). His point is to challenge the more prevalent notion that fetishism has to do with objects endowed with reified forces, a "metaphysic of alienated essence," or that it entails a passion for substance, the signified, or value. By drawing upon the etymology of "fetish," he justifies his thesis that fetishism is a "fetishism of the signifier," which he then expands to a fascination with the coherent totality of the "code" or system of signs (a veritable matrix). Cf. Jean Baudrillard, *For a Critique of the Political Economy of the Sign*, trans. Charles Levin (St. Louis: Telos, 1981), 91 *ff.*

point is, as Marx stated in his reproach to Feuerbach, not just to recognize his submission to false ideas, but to change it, to stop the humans from being happy automata and to provoke a revolt against their masters. While the Christian theme is obvious, a Platonic reading of the cave allegory would not be misplaced here, nor would reference to Descartes' evil demon that shows the subject seeking certainty an inverted world, putting all perceptual evidence into question. But these are not, at least directly, the points I will pursue. Rather, the world presented in *The Matrix* is the postmodern extension of the world of capitalism as viewed by Marx, a world equally inverted in the *camera obscura* that is the commodity form of exchange, and which equally screens the real behind the artificial illusion. This illusion as well seems completely natural. In a very general sense, Marxist fetishism is a collective Kantian adherence to the phenomenal screen and imposed ignorance of the noumenal real.

This is not, however, where Marx begins his analysis of capitalist fetishism, better known as commodity fetishism. This begins with his analysis of the commodity in the first chapter of the first volume of *Capital*, although his concern with fetishism began long before the commodity made its official appearance in this text. One finds evidence of it not only in his enduring concern with the Feuerbachian problematic of alienation as generated by religion, but as well in a confrontation with Hegel. This was not clear at first. At first, Marx simply appropriated the discourse on fetishism as found in de Brosses, although he would ironically turn the critique upon the bourgeoisie of his own society.[24] But while the critique is taken from de Brosses, his terminology is borrowed from Hegel. Marx writes:

> Fetishism is so far from raising man *above* his sensuous desires that, on the contrary, it is [as Hegel claimed] 'the *religion of sensuous desire.*' Fantasy arising from desire deceives the fetish-worshipper that an 'inanimate object' will give up its natural character in order to comply with his desires.[25]

[24] In the *Rheinische Zeitung*, Nov. 3 1842, Marx cites an episode he had read in de Brosses, but he eventually uses the scene to make an ironic reversal of the roles of the observer and observed. In this story, at a celebratory meeting between Cuban savages and Spanish colonizers, the savages, believing that gold was a fetish for the Spaniards, ceremonially threw it into the sea. De Brosses concluded that they did this out of ignorance. Anticipating his theory in *Capital*, Marx would use the story as a mirror to turn the observation of the Europeans into self-observation: the Europeans indeed had a fetish for gold, and so were no different than the savages. Cf. Iacono, 79-91.

[25] Karl Marx, "The Leading Article in No. 179 of the *Kölnische Zeitung*," in Karl Marx and Frederick Engels, *Collected Works*, Vol. 1 (New York: International, 1975), 189. Citation and context from William Pietz, "Fetishism and Materialism: The Limits of Theory in Marx," in Emily Apter and William Pietz, eds., *Fetishism as Cultural Discourse* (Ithica: Cornell University Press, 1993), 136. Hegel, in his *Lectures on the Philosophy of Religion*, sees fetishism as indicative

26

The primitive "religion of sensuous desire" is marked, as noted above, by an incapacity for abstraction (or as Hegel would say, concretion) in that it is unable to dialectically mediate naturally given immediacy with universal principles, and thus remains stuck in a purely abstract form of the concrete ("in-itself"). Sensuous immediacy for Hegel is quite simply the untrue, belonging to the development of Spirit solely as a point of departure that, in fact, falls outside of Spirit itself, as it can never be directly experienced. This blindness for directly lived sensuous experience would be the point where Marx launched his critique of Hegel's idealism, and as he did so, fetishism would at least temporarily lose some of its derogatory status.

Marx, in short, used fetishism as an illustration of a religion that addressed the substantial desires of temporally embodied individuals in order to challenge Hegel's view that individual subjects must submit their particularity to transcendent spiritual institutions. As Pietz summarizes:

> Marx's materialist critique sought to debunk the claim of universalist social institutions (the Christian church and the state) to a superior ontological status by affirming the untranscendable reality of that existential mode of particular sensuous desires and concrete, embodied individuals proper to fetish worship ...[26]

The concern with religion as an alienating phenomenon leads not only to a critique of Hegel, but as well extends the problematic found in Feuerbach's theoretical humanism: religion is nothing but a projection of the human into the heavens, but this projection in turn seems to lead an independent existence. The roles are then inverted as in a *camera obscura*, and humanity ends up kneeling to a product of its own mind, a product that seems to have lost its connection with, and leads an existence autonomous from, its producer.[27]

Feuerbach, however, only presented this problem in a formal manner pertaining to "the abstraction 'man'," and not to the historically embodied, "acutally existing, active" social being.[28] Thus, Marx found no critical

---

of "natural, immediate religion," where consciousness is still natural consciousness, "the consciousness of sensuous desire."

[26] Pietz, "Fetishism and Materialism", *op. cit.*, 142.

[27] "Consciousness can never be anything else than conscious being, and the being of men is their actual life-process. If in all ideology men and their relations appear upside-down as in a *camera obscura*, this phenomenon arises just as much from their historical life-process as the inversion of object on the retina does from their physical life process... . The phantoms formed in the brains of men [i.e. "morality, religion, metaphysics, and all the rest of ideology as well as the forms of consciousness corresponding to these"] are also, necessarily, sublimates of their material life-process." K. Marx, *The German Ideology*, vol. 1, trans. Clemens Dutt, in *Collected Works, Volume 5: Marx and Engels: 1845-47* (London: Lawrence and Wishart, 1976), 36.

[28] Ibid., 41.

approach in Feuerbach by which to actually redress this alienation. As Marx claims:

> Feuerbach starts out from the fact of religious self-estrangement, of the duplication of the world into a religious, imaginary world and a real one. His work consists in resolving the religious world into its secular basis. He overlooks the fact that after completing this work, the chief thing still remains to be done. For the fact that the secular basis lifts off from itself and establishes itself as an independent realm in the clouds can only be explained by the inner strife and intrinsic contradictoriness of this secular basis.[29]

The mere recognition of ideological forms and false consciousness alone would not resolve the problem of the apparent autonomy of the religious sphere from its human basis. Nor would it resolve the systematic oversight structuring people's behavior, the attention to things organized around a blank, a hole, from whence they arise, the Marxian unconscious. The mere concept of ideology would not reverse the alienating situation that arises from the temporal basis (i.e. the human being) having *split itself in two*: one part, the subject produced (in its objects), becoming a fixed representation (fetish) that stands over and against the other, the embodied individual, or the subject of production. The fact that what the subject has produced does not fall together with the producing subject will directly lead to fetishism, insofar as fetishism arises from the fact that the producer mistakenly perceives value as inherent in that which he or she has produced.

We are not aware of this, nevertheless we do it

It is in *Capital* that Marx systematically analyzes this split between material social action, or the real conditions of existence, and the representational forms in which this action is reflected back to humanity. He comes to see these forms not as mere ideological constructions but as real developments arising from the internal contradictions of capitalist production. Fetishism is called upon to serve as an analogy for the capitalist error of attribution, but here the error will derive from a more complicated process in which immaterial (i.e. social) value is crystallized into a material form which is then fetishistically seen as being the embodiment of that value. However, the real problem for Marx is that the notion of value itself already entails an alienating division within the process of human labor, a division specific to the capitalist form of production and based upon the internal non-equivalence of its most basic element, the commodity. What is more, the perception of value as inherent in objects, which Marx views as the core mystification of capitalism,

---

[29]   K. Marx, *Theses on Feuerbach*, *IV* (version edited by Engels) in *Collected Works Vol. 5, op.cit.*, 7.

once again testifies to the stickiness of the belief previously attributed to the "religion of sensuous desire," namely, that "an 'inanimate object' will give up its natural character in order to comply with his desires."[30]

Marx's analysis of commodity fetishism is found in the famous fourth section in the first chapter of *Capital,* "The Fetishism of Commodities and the Secret Thereof."[31] This analysis of how relations between people become relations between things is so familiar and has spawned so much comment that it hardly requires reiteration. It is here that he identifies the enigmatic, mystifying, fantastic and metaphysical vicissitudes of the commodity which "appears, at first sight, a very trivial thing" (Marx, 81), but which becomes "a mysterious thing, simply because in it the social character of men's labor appears to them as an objective character stamped upon the product of that labor" (Marx 82-3). The primary problem revealed in the fetishism that results from the production of commodities is that the human element—the qualitative differences of individual labor and the relations among people who need one another's labor, or "the social character of labor"—vanishes as if into a mist of objective appearance. It then appears as if the substance of the objects produced, namely, the labor expended to produce them, belongs not to the producers, but is rather inherent in the nature of the products, and this "appears to the producers ... to be real and final" (Marx, 85). In other words, completely natural.

At least four noteworthy transformations occur in this particular type of production process, each of which exhibits a transvaluation of commonly held notions. First, a commodity, which is nothing but a material "thing that by its properties satisfies human wants" (Marx, 45), such as iron, corn, a coat, a diamond, achieves its purpose only by being emptied of its content, its materiality evacuated. Second, material labor (skill, muscle, sweat and time) and the qualitative distinctions between different types of labor (one raises pigs, another lays bricks, another weaves clothes) attain their end when they undergo abstraction. Concrete labor is hereby reduced to an "unsubstantial reality," namely, homogeneous human labor or the paradoxical notion of a "social [i.e. unsubstantial] substance" (Marx, 57). This type of 'substance' is

---

[30]   In Auguste Comte's view, it is precisely the intimate connection of the subject and the external world characteristic of *fétichisme* that calls for a new appreciation of this outdated mode of religion: "All the observable bodies thus being immediately personified ... the exterior world spontaneously presents itself in a *perfect harmony with the spectator,* which has never since been retrieved to the same degree, and which should produce in him *a special feeling of complete satisfaction...*", in A. Comte, *Oeuvres d'Auguste Comte* Vol. 5, *Cours de Philosophie Positive,* 5th edition (Paris: Au Siège de la Société Positiviste, 1894), 36, emphasis added.

[31]   K. Marx, *Capital: A Critique of Political Economy* Vol. 1, in *Collected Works Vol. 35* (London : Lawrence and Wishart, 1996), 81-94. Further reference to *Capital* will be indicated (Marx), followed by page number.

otherwise known as "value."[32] With the first two moves of capitalist production the physical form of substance withdraws and the value form emerges.

The value form emerges when—and this is the third step—these material realities emptied of their content are re-materialized in a commodity to be exchanged. As Marx states, "When looked at as crystals of this social substance, common to them all [i.e. homogeneous human labor], they are— Values... . the common substance that manifests itself in the exchange value of commodities ... is their value... . exchange value is the only form in which the value of commodities can manifest itself of be expressed" (Marx, 48). The third step re-embodies disembodied substance. It then seems, as noted above, that each of these valued objects (commodities) has an inherently distinct value; that they are valuable in themselves, for what they are. This is the first step of fetishism.

Finally, given the unruly, though only apparent, heterogeneity of all these different objects, it would be impossible to exchange them should some common measure not be established by which to do so. Now, this common measure or "universal equivalent" should be recognized as human labor, but this has vanished from sight. Human labor, after having scattered itself into the diverse physical objects where it lies shrouded and unrecognized, is transubstantiated into a single holy commodity where the essence of all value is embodied—money. Money becomes the fetish of capitalist society, the *Ersatz* that obscures its function as *Ersatz* and becomes the *Ding-an-sich*, animated with a mysterious life of its own as interest-bearing money-capital. "It is in *interest-bearing capital* ... that capital finds its most objectified form, its pure fetish form... . Capital—as an entity—appears here as an independent source of value."[33] To state the issue in highly applicable religious terminology, money, which is in effect the *incarnans* of socially necessary labor time—the *incarnatum*—is not revered because it is recognized as the materialization of the real source of meaning, rather it draws everything into

---

[32] "The value of commodities is the very opposite of the coarse materiality of their substance, not an atom of matter enters into its composition. Turn and examine a single commodity ... yet in so far as it remains an object of value, it seems impossible to grasp it," (Marx, 57). Everyone knows of Marx's distinction between use value and exchange value. Use value is quite simply the usefulness of a thing for a certain need and constituted by its immediate consumption, while exchange value is quantitative amount of one thing needed to acquire another, and therefore expresses nothing intrinsic about the thing at all. Use value sticks to the commodity; exchange value is separable from it. When I write "value" then, this should be read as exchange value.

[33] K. Marx, *Theories of Surplus Value*, part 3, trans. Jack Cohen and S. W. Ryazanskaya (Moscow : Progress, 1971), 494, 498. Cited in Pietz, "Fetishism and Materialism" *op.cit.*, 149. Pietz here draws an analogy between the mystery of capitalist society and "the mystery of the Catholic church as the body of Christ is concentrated and expressed in the sacrament of the Eucharist..."

itself, erasing its referential structure. Money, in reality a social construction, an abstraction that serves as a means to satisfy real desires, comes to be desired in itself—as if it were a substance. For, by possessing money, one has the source of all value, as was said of the primitives, in one's pocket. Enough money should suffice to cover any lack, to fulfill the dream of self-sufficiency.

We have briefly seen how Marx, as in *The Matrix*, presents the process of fetishism in the capitalist system of production as casting a veil over the real relations of production, blocking access to reality and mystifying people as to what they are desiring when they desire commodities. This mystification, however, is not experienced as confusing. Rather, it is a form of non-knowledge that clears a path for enjoyment within alienation, insofar as it allows people to overlook ugly matters such as the inequality between waged labor and surplus revenue, matters which, if recognized, could hinder their enjoyment of the benefits of capitalism. And again, as in *The Matrix*, when experienced from within the system this general fetishism seems completely natural, and so goes unnoticed. It is getting out, or waking up and exiting the system, which is dangerous.

Now, there has been no lack of criticism of Marx's humanistic ontology of base and superstructure, of a signified (human labor or utility) distinct from signification (exchange and appearance). Indeed, Marx's critique of the mystifying dissimulation that the exchange of commodities and money exerts on the human relations at their foundation has led to him being accused of having a fetish for substance and essence, as well as for the purely rational economic subject. It is he, and the notion of fetishism he inherited from the Enlightenment, who is the primary target when Baudrillard claims that "the metaphor of fetishism, wherever it appears, involves a fetishization of the conscious subject or of human essence, a rationalist metaphysic that is at the root of the whole system of occidental Christian values."[34] Indeed, Marx did posit that there have been and could still be transparent societies of rational economic individuals whose relations are not distorted by the type of inversions that occur when individuals relate to one another through their commodities. Consequently, in the absence of commodities, and hence of the capitalist system, social relations should cast off their religious and fetishistic reifications. We know this is not the case.

In order to move forward, I would like to briefly reverse directions and examine not the advanced analysis of commodity fetishism, but the very core of it, that ambiguous object called the commodity. Now, in the fourth section of *Capital*, Marx says that, "value [the form of the commodity in exchange] ... converts every product into a social hieroglyphic. Later on, we try to decipher the hieroglyphic to get behind the secret of our own social products ..." (Marx, 85). Now, at first glance it appears that he is saying that we will try to find the true secret (labor) behind the false form (exchange value of the commodity),

---

[34] J. Baudrillard, "Fetishism and Ideology", *op. cit.*, 89.

thereby confirming the separation of essence/signified and appearance/ signifier, with the latter obscuring the former. But if we look more closely, it seems rather that the "secret" to which he is referring is not something hidden, but is rather *the form itself*. If so, it would then seem that in capitalist production, as in a dream, the form in which the commodity appears does not hide some determinate content which exists independently from the form, but rather that form is, *at least in a partial way*, the content. The latent is there in the manifest. This allows it to veil that other scene where the remainder of the content resides, and which will never come into view. Fetishism is the result of this split. This speculation may be justified, I believe, by noting that there is a structural hollow in the foundation stone of capital—the commodity—which we will find again in Freud's late theory of fetishism, and by extension, in Lacan's notions of castration and the *objet a*. A brief examination of the commodity will point the way.

The Commodity and a Case of Foot Fetishism

In the opening paragraphs of *Capital*, Marx establishes the dynamic of the commodity. It is a thing of use, it has a utility which "makes it a use value," (Marx, 46). Utility, Marx says, is "not a thing of air," but has physical properties, materiality. This materiality, however, is only realized in use or consumption. And, as Marx states and Keenan[35] emphasizes, there are many different uses for this material: commodities are thus not only their material embodiment, but are the "material depositories of exchange value," exchange value that liquidates them as materials. A commodity is therefore both raw materiality/material human labor and an empty "site." Many qualities or uses may be inscribed within this site, and this inscription only takes place, or may only be perceived, when it takes the form of an object to be exchanged.

Use value is therefore not the metaphysical unity or material ground that it is made out to be.[36] Matter/labor is not a force or a ground, but is a sort of phantasm that takes shape in a metonymical series of exchanges, as a commodity can be exchanged again and again for any other object on the premise that they all contain within them the same ghostly, abstract substance that has been subtracted from the human being: one's labor power ... or the mother's breast.[37] Objects may be exchanged on the premise that every object

---

[35] Thomas Keenan, "The Point is to Exchange it," in *Fetishism as Cultural Discourse, op. cit.*, 160-1.
[36] Ibid., 161.
[37] "It [the *objet a*] is precisely what is subtracted from the living being... . it is of this that all the forms of the *objet a* ... are the representatives, the equivalents. The *objets a* are merely its representatives, its figures. The breast ... certainly represents that part of himself that the individual loses at birth, and which may serve to symbolize the most profound lost object," Jacques Lacan, *The Four*

can substitute for this phantasmagoria called "socially necessary labor time." Every particular commodity amounts to a reification of this "substance." They obscure it even while they arise from it. "In this respect," according to Henry Krips in his Lacanian reading of fetishism, "the *objet a* bears a structural similarity to the 'commodity': it is not only a concrete object but also a ghostly value, a false essence carried by the concrete object and constituted through the processes of exchange."[38] I will discuss this further in the closing section. While reflecting on this ambiguous structure of the commodity, however, I was struck by its similarity to Freud's second attempt to analyze fetishism, as found in a short paper delivered to the Vienna Psychoanalytic Society in 1909, "On the Genesis of Fetishism,"[39] where he introduces the concept of "partial repression."

Freud's short text seems quite straightforward and self-contained. The arrival of an original concept occurs without any fanfare. First of all, I note that Freud has entirely changed his idea regarding the origin of fetishism as described in his *Three Essays on the Theory of Sexuality* (1905).[40] Here, in brief, he assumes from Binet the explanation that fetishism is a phenomenon acquired in early childhood through a coincidental association of a circumstantial factor with a sexual excitation. This coincidence creates a lasting impression and is later, in adult life, activated by means of reminiscence. In 1909, he claims that "fetishism does not derive from a reminiscence, but ... a repression of instinct [has] occurred."[41] This is no ordinary repression. Rather, it is "a type of repression which is instituted by the splitting of the [instinctual-representational] complex. A portion is genuinely repressed, while the other portion is idealized ... [and] raised to a fetish."[42] Two examples from a single case of perversion are used to illustrate this schema.

Fundamental Concepts of Psychoanalysis, ed. Jacques-Alain Miller, trans. Alan Sheridan (New York: Norton, 1981), 198. This reference will be clarified as we continue.

[38] Henry Krips, *Fetishism: An Erotics of Culture*, (Ithica: Cornell University Press, 1999), 21.

[39] Sigmund Freud, "On the Genesis of Fetishism," in "Freud and Fetishism: Previously Unpublished Minutes of the Vienna Psychoanalytic Society," ed. and trans. Louis Rose, *Psychoanalytic Quarterly LVII*, 1988, (147-166). This text received little attention prior to Henry Rey-Flaud's exhaustive study published in 1994, *Comment Freud inventa le féthichisme ... et réinventa la psychanalyse*, (Paris: Èditions Payot et Rivages, 1994).

[40] S. Freud, *Three Essays on the Theory of Sexuality*, SE VII. This text went through a series of revisions from the time of its publication until 1920, so what I am presenting is an extreme reduction. For further commentary, see Paul Moyaert's "Fetishism and the Vicissitudes of the Object in Sublimation According to Freud and Lacan" and Andreas De Block's "Genital Constructions: A Critique of Freud's 'Fetishism'," also in this volume.

[41] S. Freud, "On the Genesis of Fetishism," 155.

[42] Ibid. Freud asserts that this is nothing new, and illustrates with reference to the cult of the Virgin: if sensuality is repressed and women are degraded, this

The first details the creation of clothes fetishism. As a child, the patient regularly witnessed his mother undressing, and subsequently became a voyeur. He was stimulated by watching women undress, the goal being to see the naked body, and the final gesture prior to the ultimate revelation, the removal of the pants, became the most significant. At issue, as Freud clarifies, is the drive (desire) to look—scopophilia. Owing to a prohibition, this desire is repressed, but what transpires next is quite strange: that which formerly *prevented* him from seeing the naked truth, namely, clothing, is now "worship[ped]."[43] Freud concludes, *"He becomes a clothes fetishist out of the repression of the desire to look."*[44] We should at least provisionally be able to detect the Marxian dynamic of commodity fetishism here, insofar as the commodity, which veils the real relations between people, becomes desired and worshipped as if it is the bearer of an intrinsic value. That which hides the real becomes revered. Let us move on to the second example, which will serve as our primary reference point.

The patient's perversion has now changed from clothes fetishism to boot fetishism. In this case the schema also involves a primitive satisfaction and its repression, but here the pleasure derives from (unsavory) smells—coprophilia. The source of this smell is the foot.[45] The representational complex is the smell (use value) and the foot (the form it takes, or exchange value). This complex, adhering to one and the same commodity (the foot), is then split apart, or undergoes partial repression: "the pleasure from odors is suppressed, while the odorless foot is idealized. In the ideal, odor is no longer an issue."[46] Freud continues: "Here we find again a lost instinctual pleasure, but here the

requires a complementary idealization of the mother as the Virgin Mary. A similar structure is found in the bipartition of the sexual object in the attempt to subvert the incest prohibition, and thus to artfully dodge the anxiety of castration. If the overestimation of the loved object is derivative from the oedipal fixation on the mother, then the incest prohibition requires that the loved object be spared from sexual relations. Barring a solution, the subject must renounce sexual satisfaction. It is thus better to split the mother into two women: one's partner, from whom sexual enjoyment is detached, and who thus remains pure and deserving of tender respect; and a mistress who is not respected, and is thus the outlet for sexual satisfaction without fear of violating the prohibition. The fetish is a solution that renders the bipartition of the woman redundant—one satisfies oneself with the fetish instead of the woman.

[43] Ibid., 155. A similar explanation is provided in a footnote to the *Three Essays* added in 1915: speaking of cases of foot-fetishism, Freud claims that "the scopophilic instinct, seeking to reach its object (originally the genitals) from underneath, was *brought to a halt* in its pathway by prohibition and repression. For this reason it became attached to a fetish in the form of a foot or shoe...", 68, emphasis added.

[44] Ibid., author's emphasis.

[45] Out of concern for brevity, I will forgo the explanation of how olfactory pleasure derives from the primitive anal object, excrement.

[46] Ibid., 157.

direct object [the foot] of its complex is separated from the instinct and rises to a fetish. This is, in essence, the novelty."[47] The foot, as we saw with the commodity, has been devalued (stripped of its significant qualities, its odor), and revalued ("rises to a fetish"). The very attribute that had made the foot valuable as a source of pleasure has been lost, illustrating a process quite faithful to the type of alchemy generating the commodity. The sexual aim of the drive (or human labor) is subject to repression, yet finds another path for satisfaction by transforming the aim into a form of cultural production, namely, the foot (the commodity), which will pass along the chain of signification and be exchanged for another commodity, the boot.

The commodities that are fetishized, the foot and the boot, are theoretically interchangeable because they both derive from an essence that has been lost: the pleasure derived from smells. The congruence is thus as follows: the commodity (the foot or the boot) no longer contains all the attributes that provide an object with intrinsic value. In fact, we are now dealing with a purified foot, a foot without qualities, a foot which is nothing but the absence of the foot, a "disincarnated incarnation of substance,"[48] an illusion, a phantom. How then is one to account for the gravitational pull that the fetishized commodity-foot still exerts on the subject? How can this supremely contradictory object—this object full of content, yet effectively empty; a site of lack, yet materially embodied—come to be desired so intensely? This is what remains for us to answer.

3. Disavowal: The Artful Dodge

The two approaches to fetishism detailed thus far seem to be divergent in orientation and indicative of an impasse as to whether fetishism is a matter of an individual's overly intense attachment to the concrete, or an endemic tendency of our socio-economic system to mislead through appearances. In fact, however, they seem to effectively revolve around the same classic problematic of fetishism indicated at the start of this essay: the substitution of one thing for something else, and the false attribution to that substitute of powers and qualities it does not have. Thus, while we have been able to designate the general structure of fetishism and how it is likely to occur, little solid evidence regarding specifically why it occurs or whether there is an alternative to the classic structure has been established. In a sense then, it has retained little more than its metaphorical determination, and is still an incomparably migratory phenomenon. Yet, with the dynamic of partial repression, and our brief reference to the phantasmic density of the *objet a*, we

---

[47] Ibid., author's emphasis.
[48] H. Rey-Flaud, *op. cit.*, 93.

have at least entered a path that may lead us forward. To make our next step, let us once again enter *The Matrix*.

There is a scene in *The Matrix* that breaks with its dualistic structure of those in the truth and those prey to illusion, for here we find someone straddling both sides. It concerns a character, interchangeably Judas or Faust, who has escaped his computer-generated prison of the matrix but feels equally imprisoned by the diversion-free drudgery and revolutionary seriousness that is his life in "the desert of the real," where food is but an amorphous bowl of sloppy nourishment and all the illusory accoutrements of capitalist society are not only considered opiates for the slumbering unenlightened, but are also, in reality, simply unavailable. This character (Cypher) is enlisted by the defenders of the matrix to betray Neo, the potential liberator of the human race, so that they may eliminate him. The reward for his betrayal is getting plugged back into an illusory, yet libidinal, life in the matrix. The meeting to secure the deal occurs in an exquisite, computer-generated restaurant, where Cypher is dining on fine wine and a juicy steak, and enjoying it immensely. Now, at this moment, Cypher is in the fetishistic zone: he is still aware of the distinction between the real world in which he had been living and the illusory world in which he is currently dining, yet this knowledge does not temper his enjoyment.

While eating the steak, which he in fact knows is nothing but the same bowl of grey gruel he has been eating for years—if he is indeed eating anything at all—he tells the policeman/Caiaphas/Mephistopheles figure (approximately) the following: "I know when I'm putting this in my mouth, the matrix is telling my brain it's juicy and delicious ... (chews away) ... but goddamn it tastes good." That is, he knows very well that he is not receiving pleasure from any real substance, yet he enjoys it all the same. He knows that exchange value is not intrinsic value, but this knowledge does not alter his practical behavior. He knows that the real is not going to conform to his desires or expectations, and thus he implicitly knows that his desires are unsatisfiable in the real world. He therefore seeks refuge in the imaginary world where the lack of satisfaction can be numbed, his disbelief in the false world of the matrix suspended by the modicum of satisfaction that the illusion provides.

Now, this scene illustrates what has been accepted as the classic, contemporary definition of the fetishistic attitude as pronounced by Octave Mannoni in his article, "Je sais bien, mais quand même" (I know very well, but all the same), a formula derived from Freud's concept of disavowal (*Verleugnung*). Disavowal is the simultaneous denial and avowal of castration, introduced in his "Fetishism" from 1927. Here, with the concepts of disavowal and castration, Freud's approach to fetishism takes a final twist, though the transformation from missing substance to object, Thing to thing, remains relatively unaltered. The psychodynamic operation guiding this trans-formation, however, for the first time becomes more transparent, which is not to say that the ambiguity of fetishism is resolved. Indeed, disavowal, the concept at the core of Freud's new approach, is ambivalence itself. It testifies to a split in the subject on the basis of a simultaneous acknowledgment and denial of something that has (not) been perceived: specifically, the maternal penis. In lieu of a decision being taken as to the presence or absence of this "particular and quite special penis,"[49] the subject creates a fetish, allowing him to have it both ways.

Freud's first move in this text explains what he now expects to be the solution to every case of fetishism: the fetish does not take the place of a person who is unattainable, nor does it derive from a repressed instinct, rather, it is a substitute for the penis of the female, which it is "designed to preserve from extinction."[50] One cannot fail to be struck by how curious this formulation is, insofar as it claims that one is trying to preserve something that *is not there* from being lost. To clarify this aberration, we must see that something else is at issue, namely, the boy's *belief* in this prized object, his narcissistic *expectation* that everyone is the same as he is, and therefore has a penis like he does. The problem is that his actual perception contradicts the belief that he does not want to relinquish, for if her penis—which must have been there—is missing, then his own could be in danger. How does the child deal with this problem?

Freud's first suggestion is that "the boy refused to take cognizance of the fact of his having perceived that a woman does not possess a penis."[51] Just as soon as he has proposed this explanation, however, he dismisses it in favor of a better one:

> In the situation we are considering ... we see that the perception has persisted, and that a very energetic action has been undertaken to maintain the disavowal. It is not true that ... he has preserved unaltered his belief that women have a phallus. *He has retained that belief, but he has also given it up.*[52]

We clearly cannot claim that the child retains his belief out of ignorance. We cannot say that he *does not know* that the woman does not have a penis, that the steak is not real, that commodities are not inherently valuable. Rather, because of the implied threat to his own penis and the subsequent doubt as to it remaining in his possession, he simply prefers it otherwise. Thus, to avoid facing the threat of castration, and in an attempt to neutralize the conflict between his new knowledge and his previous belief, he *fabricates (facere)* an *artificial (factitium)* sense of certainty by turning away from reality. Like a little Cartesian attempting to find some indubitable ground, he mistrusts that

---

49 S. Freud, *SE XXI*, 152.
50 Ibid.
51 Ibid., 153.
52 Ibid., 154, emphasis added.

which appears to his senses and founds his certainty on what he cannot see, but which must nevertheless exist.

The reason for this preference, however, casts a whole new perspective on the fetish, and changes its symbolic status: the child experiences castration *anxiety* at the perception of the lack, and the fetish is created *to defend against the anxiety* generated by his perception, functioning as a sort of a screen against the unwelcome information. At the same time, however, it erects a "memorial" to the lack in order to testify to its enduring presence. The fetish, let us be clear, not only serves to *disavow* a lack and assert a presence, but as well to *incarnate* a lack, to simultaneously veil and unveil an essential absence. This is the new function of the fetish. Taken strictly in these terms, however, this function would seem restricted to the repair of phallic damage, and would be limited to a male phenomenon. By denying the apparent loss suffered by the female, the male child can rest assured that he will not suffer a similar loss. By detaching the phallus from the female through the creation of the fetish-memorial, he can both preserve her lack and keep her phallus, thereby making possible a "normal" sexual life. That is, he will not have to desire phallic partners, but can pretend to desire female partners because the real source of his pleasure, the phallus, is in his hands. In effect, the revelation that should have jarred his belief in the phallic woman has only succeeded in reinstating that belief in another form. He thus retains his belief despite his knowledge.[53] But if we are to push our analysis beyond the question of phallic integrity, which would severely limit rather than expand the approach to fetishism, we must read disavowal in a broader sense.

For the moment, let us stay within the dynamic of disavowal in the mother-child relation. We may initially identify the mother at two developmental points that are "violently in conflict and nevertheless welded together."[54] We first find her on the "archaic" level, as the child's original object of satisfaction, a totality with which the child exists as in a state of unity without fissure, primary narcissism or simply "l'*être* par excellence." The mother allows the child to feel omnipotent by providing the illusion that external reality (the breast) is at the child's command.[55] Then, after a period of the child's separation from her, we have the mother as discovered to have no phallus, as being simply the site for an "observation of a fundamental lack ... of *non-avoir* par excellence."[56] The fetish then, as we have seen particularly with the commodity but also with the boxer's watch, would serve to coalesce

[53]   This is the main point of Mannoni's essay. Despite knowledge (je sais bien) one still believes (mais quand même). Cf. Octave Mannoni, "Je sais bien, mais quand même... ", in *Clefs pour l'imaginaire* (Paris: Seuil, 1969), 9-33.

[54]   This quote and following from Roger Dadoun, "Le Fétichisme dans le film d'horreur," in *Objets du fétichisme, op. cit.*, 230.

[55]   Cf. D.W. Winnicott, "Transitional Objects and Transitional Phenomena," *International Journal of Psychoanalysis*, 34, (1953) 88-97.

[56]   R. Dadoun, *op. cit.*, 231.

these two moments into a single object, an object composed of an ambiguous coincidence of a fullness of being and an essential emptiness. There where one expects to find substance, essence, and ultimately satisfaction, one encounters a lack. Expectation of satisfaction is thwarted, and this is perceived as intolerable. Now, it is tempting to say that the fetish, in its gesture of imposing the *non-savoir* of this *non-avoir*, simply returns the phallus to the mother and reinstates the illusion of her wholeness, from which follows the reinstatement of the child's belief in a beneficent totality. But while it may be the case that the fetish is the symbolic representative of the maternal penis, it is not necessarily so.

Rather, and in a much more general sense, the fetish inhabits the empty space, a space opened up by the demise of primary narcissism and the resulting non-coincidence of the original object and the subject separated from the source of archaic plenitude. Now, as we know from Lacan, the first 'object' to occupy this space is the mirror, or rather, the self-reflection that reassembles the broken totality of primary narcissism by offering the newly isolated subject an image of its own stability, albeit in a fictional direction. While this new unity is thoroughly enjoyable insofar as it revives the pleasure of primary narcissism, the price of the imaginary construction of the ego and the reestablishment of (secondary) narcissism is alienation, the bifurcation of the subject into its bodily existence and its virtual unity—a splitting inherited from Freud. Castration anxiety now becomes a conflict internal to the subject, a fantasy of the dismemberment of the newly constructed image of bodily integrity, death by dissatisfaction. The denial of castration would thus amount to a cathexis of an image of wholeness, something like the fantasy of the phallic mother. Avowal of castration may then be read as *coming to terms with the loss* of the totally satisfying object by means of symbolic mediation.[57] The fetishistic mediation of castration, on the contrary, begs the question of the loss, blocking it from view.

My concern, however, is how the lack of coincidence between particular objects and the missing Object plays itself out on the field of desire. Indeed, this lack of coincidence is not only the very origin of anxiety, but also of desire. Now, if we take desire in general as modeled on the search for the lost intimacy of the primordial mother-child relation, and we know that this intimacy can never be restored, then we may posit that desire searches for a totally satisfying something, though it is satisfied with nothing; that in fact it searches for Nothing, and is thus unsatisfiable. Nothingness, however, cannot dispense with its signs, without which it could never be desired. Desire cannot have nothingness as its direct object, and so it searches the world of objects for

---

[57] I have in mind particularly the mediation found in the *Fort-Da* game, the drama of the mother's presence and absence played out by the child who substitutes a bobbin for the mother. The child repeats her comings and goings by tossing the bobbin away, and reeling it back in with the string.

a figure that may repair the broken identity, the lost intimacy. The objects of desire, however, are structurally split in the same manner as the subject. Namely, they are external appearance, the outward form of their embodied substance, and yet this embodiment disguises their internal lack or negativity insofar as they are but echoes of the original lost body or substance from which they have been detached. While offering a promise of regained wholeness, they nevertheless consist of a void that no distinct object can fill, and withdraw from grasp. Hence, therefore, the ultimate dissatisfaction of desire: because of the impossible equivalence between the object and the Thing (the primordially lost object), no object can yield to the subject the Thing that lies both within the subject itself, as its irretrievable past, and in the object of desire. Acceptance of dissatisfaction—of the fact that despite all one's efforts, one will never fall together with oneself, insofar as the totally satisfying object is impossible—is essentially a realization of finitude. Thus, the avowal of finitude may be roughly equated to the avowal of castration.

The ambiguity internal to the object of desire, however, effectively paves the way for the cunning of the fetishist, the *artful dodge of desire,* and the *disavowal of finitude.* We have said that the fetishist denies a lack by producing a fetish. With this gesture, the fetishist also denies the anguish of non-coincidence which leaves the subject prey to a desire that cannot be satisfied, and thus prey to its finitude. The fetish, like any object of desire, is both more and less than an object. As an embodied figure, it embodies the imaginary dream of a satisfaction that would cancel desire. As a locus of lack, it signifies that desire is unsatisfiable. The fetish is empty, and so the locus of a radical negativity without objective content; yet it takes a substantial form that fascinates the desiring subject, arousing the expectation that what has been lost can be regained. The fetish, however, like the object of desire, is ultimately deceptive. It is a veil that provides the false intimation that there is actually something substantial to be attained beneath its phenomenal appearance, the desire for which keeps the negativity of desire in motion. It is an enchanting veil that absorbs the subject's attention, a veil negating itself as a veil by falsely presenting itself as the fulfillment of what it can only promise. In this way, fixation on the fetish is a way to deny the intrinsic dissatisfaction of desire, effectively calling the dialectic of desire to a standstill.[58] By placing an object between oneself and the anxious emptiness of pure desire, one avoids the confrontation with desire's infinitude, and avoids one's finitude in the process.

---

[58] This notion is consistent with one of the central points of Krips' Lacanian reading of fetishism, namely, that the fetish is pleasurable precisely insofar as it prevents the subject from accessing its desire. The fetishist, in short, prefers to engage *the obstacle* to the fulfilment of desire, rather than pursuing what is really desired.

I believe that the aetiology I have just illustrated goes some way to clarifying the "why?" of fetishism, but I do not believe that it adequately explains the wider reasons for the fetishistic impulse, nor the uniqueness of the phenomenon. For, as thus far presented, it would be difficult to distinguish a fetish from any other object of desire. And indeed, it ultimately may be difficult to do so. Yet fetishism entails an even more artful solution to the question of desire than I have thus far indicated. It is the artfulness of the "*mais quand même*," in which expectation of satisfaction persists *despite*, or perhaps because of, dis-illusionment with respect to its possible attainment. Compare this with the phenomenon of being in love. When initially in love, the love object is so overvalued that one cannot imagine that the feeling of being in love experienced with that particular person could be duplicated with any other person. The exclusivity of falling in love may be called fetishistic: beyond all reason, one focuses on this one individual as the embodiment of all of one's expectations of fulfillment. The person is irreplaceable. In the course of a healthy loving relationship, however, the loved person is gradually dissociated from one's own happiness, in the sense that the loved person does not remain the direct object of one's hopes for fulfillment. One does recognize that one could just as well love someone else, but this does not take away the significance of the loved person. The mystery of fetishism is that the closed circuit of desire and the belief in the satisfying nature of the object of may be shattered, and consciously so, but the belief in the exclusive fulfilling object remains, despite.

Recall the figure from *The Matrix* (Cypher) who was straddling the fetishistic divide between a sober, conscious world and a world of enchant-ment. There is one final aspect of Cypher's choice to take flight from his barren world by reentering the matrix that may help illuminate the broader sense of the fetishistic disavowal than the one with which we have been working. Cypher's life in the disenchanted real world was turned upside-down by the arrival of the chosen one who received everyone's attention. This included the attentions of the lone female in their group, whom had consistently rejected Cypher's amorous advances. Cypher wants to be what she wants, but she seems disinterested in the phallus, at least until the chosen one comes along.

This wound to his narcissism unleashes a jealousy that not only motivates his betrayal, but also his flight from the barren real and into the everyday, capitalistic world of the matrix. In short, he refuses to accept symbolic castration: he refuses to come to terms with what he is not or does not have, and what he is not or does not have is what he believes to be the focus of her desire, whatever that may be. He is at a loss as to how to attain the object of his desire, for the attainment of his desire depends on factors both outside of his control, and outside of his knowledge: there is no way to know how to become the focus of someone else's desire, or if one already is that focus, one will never know why. And this, of course, makes the inherently narcissistic ego, the first line of defense against uncertainty and the executor of the drive to self-mastery, feel quite vulnerable and anxious. Consequently, when Cypher makes the deal to secure his entrance back into the matrix, we see an attempt to protect his ego and to regain a sense of control over the satisfaction of his desires. He requests that in his new fantasy-life, he will be "someone important," someone rich, desirable, phallic ... in short, he wishes to have and be everything, to beg the question of his phallic sufficiency and unburden himself of the weight of finitude.

In fact then, what he really wants is for reality to conform to his desires, in fulfillment of his narcissistic expectations. His decision to opt for a fictional scenario rather than reality shows the persistence of the pre-enlightened attitude that the world can be magically influenced by our actions. But reality is never so accommodating, nor desire so definite, for this gap between desire and a satisfying reality to be closed. Desire is born and lives in this lack of coincidence between an amorphous expectation of satisfaction and the object in which one seeks to secure that satisfaction. It depends on this lack of coincidence for its life. And it is precisely this gap that our fetishistic subject endeavors to close, even if this requires fixation on an imaginary scenario to trap ones desire.

A similar scenario is presented in Mannoni's article ("Je sais bien ..."). I am not referring to his primary analysis of the ritual belief of the Hopi Indians, but rather to two everyday occurrences. The first concerns a horoscope. Every reasonable person should know that horoscopes are nothing more than diversionary fictions. It stretches the imagination to think that one could rely on them. But suppose that one has already made unalterable plans for the day, such as moving to a new house, and then reads a horoscope that, while utterly vague, just happens to suggest some direct relevance to one's situation, something like, "Neptune interfering with Jupiter. Bad day for making a big move. Stay put for now. You may be rewarded for doing so." Now, while this horoscope could refer to just about anything, the coincidence with the fact that one is in fact moving on that day produces a form of enjoyment, perhaps laughter. The coincidence has no meaning, but it is nevertheless enjoyable.

The second example is a story Mannoni relates from his own psycho-analytic practice, and hinges on a simple error. A patient phoned Mannoni, but his secretary wrote the patient's name incorrectly. The name written down, however, does resemble that of a friend of Mannoni (a black musician) from whom he was expecting a visit. Mannoni thus instructs his secretary to have the person come at once, so that they would have time for an apéritif. It is of course the patient, and not the black musician, who shows up at Mannoni's door, and so Mannoni immediately recognizes his error. He decides, however, to act as if no mistake has been made, so as to determine whether the patient would fall back into the proper analytic situation despite the obvious misunderstanding. He was pleased to find that the patient did just that. It is only later that Mannoni, having paid careful attention to the patient's first words, discovers the fruitful lesson from this mistake. The patient: "I know very well that that was a joke about the apéritif. But just the same, it made me quite happy." Now, the patient indeed recognized that an error had been made, that the famous analyst was not actually asking him to come over for a drink. Nevertheless, and regardless how unlikely that would be, he is disappointed, for it would be quite satisfying to think that Mannoni indeed wanted to have a casual drink with him. An ingenious solution, however, is forthcoming: the patient claims not to have believed for a second in what he had briefly hoped, but rather says, "My wife, she believed it."

The primary lesson Mannoni illustrates is how belief can survive its own denial by reality, that belief can persist even after the believer has been disillusioned, and therefore knows the belief is false. Belief persists, that is, without the subject even knowing about it, simply because of a projection that allows someone else to believe in one's place. On the one hand, this indicates how, in Lacan's playful phraseology, *"les non-dupes errent,"*[59] how the ones who believe themselves to be in possession of the truth (*les non-dupes*) still may be lead astray by their own desires (*errent*). On the other hand, this structure of belief essentially relieves the subject from the responsibility for its own self-deception. Yet the potential benefits of this apparent paradox, a paradox that may very well be "at the base of our human existence," are substantial.

The paradox allows the subject to occupy, *without internal conflict*, the fetishistic zone between clear, rational consciousness and an enchanted, symbolic world. That is, one may be enlightened, irreligious, and exhibit an efficient pragmatic rationale, and yet at the same time be involved in a symbolic world where things acquire an excessive significance. As long as one disavows one's own belief, and projects it onto someone or something else that embodies this belief in one's place, one can effectively have it both ways: one can assume one's tiny allotted place in the anonymous, profane world of senseless work and formal responsibilities, one can live within the mundane limits of the techno-industrial suburban landscape, and at the same time escape those limits, *despite oneself.* Fetishism plays on this boundary where one simultaneously tries to be oneself and escape oneself, insofar as it somehow answers the very legitimate, and perhaps unavoidable, desire to have one's personal attachments take on a deeper symbolic significance. It thus represents an all-too-human attempt to restore enough meaning in our relation with the world to hide the potential groundlessness of our everyday endeavors. It reveals an attempt to give the everyday a sense of the extraordinary.

---

[59] Cf. J. Lacan, *Le Seminaire. Livre XXI. Les non-dupes errent/Les noms du père, 1973-74*, unpublished. This phrase is a linguistic and aural pun on the name of the father, "le nom du père" and the "no" of the father, "le non du père." Thus, we read "le non (du p)ère" = "les non-dupes errent."

FETISHISM AND THE VICISSITUDES OF THE OBJECT IN SUBLIMATION ACCORDING TO FREUD AND LACAN

Paul Moyaert

Freud defines sublimation as follows: "This capacity to exchange its originally sexual aim for another one, which is no longer sexual but which is psychically related to the first aim, is called the capacity for *sublimation*."[1] By aim Freud understands the action that incites the instinct. The aim of the instinct is to arrive at an action that results in a perceptible decrease in tension. Basically, sublimation does something to the aim of the instinct: the instincts turn away from their sexual aim, which is simultaneously transformed into a new, non-sexual aim. But does something also happen to the object of the instinct in sublimation? Does sublimation necessarily go together with a change on the side of the object-pole of the instinct? If so, what sort of change is required for sublimation? Can the object also play an active role in the generation of sublimation?

In the *New Introductory Lectures on Psychoanalysis*, Freud says the following about the vicissitude of the object in sublimation: "A certain kind of modification of the aim and *change of the object*, in which our social valuation is taken into account, is described by us as 'sublimation'."[2] It is not clear whether Freud is referring here to one or two changes. In any case, what is certain is the following. Sublimation changes the function of the object with respect to the function it had previously served in sexual life. Sublimation generates a product that, without answering directly to vital and sexual needs, may still be satisfying and socially valued, and thus also be validated.

> One thing only alludes to the possibility of the happy satisfaction of the instinct, and that is the notion of sublimation. But it is clear that if one looks at the most esoteric formulation of the concept in Freud, in the context of his representing it as realized pre-eminently in the activity of the artist, it literally means that man has the possibility of making his desires tradable or saleable in the form of products. The frankness and even cynicism of such a formulation

---

[1] Sigmund Freud, "'Civilized' Sexual Morality and Modern Nervous Illness,' *SE IX*, 187.

[2] Freud, *New Introductory Lectures on Psychoanalysis, SE XXII*, 97, emphasis added. In "Two Encyclopaedia Articles," the review article that Freud wrote for the *Handwörterbuch der Sexualwissenschaften*, the definition is as follows: "The most important vicissitude which an instinct can undergo seems to be *sublimation*; here both object and aim are changed, so that what was originally a sexual instinct finds satisfaction in some achievement which is no longer sexual but has a higher social or ethical valuation", *SE XVIII*, 256.

has in my eyes a great merit, although it is far from exhausting the fundamental question, and that is, how is it possible.[3]

Social valuation, whether expressed in hard currency or not, does not suffice to define a sublimated instinct. For, not everything that is socially valued is deserving of the name sublimation, and that which receives no social valuation is not necessarily excluded from sublimation. This does not change the fact that it is still advisable, as Lacan suggests, to consider social valuation as an important element in sublimation. But the connection with social valuation should then be relaxed in the following way: what is not *amenable* to social valuation is not eligible for sublimation. Neither actual recognition, nor the lack of it, is thus a decisive criterion. When Lacan refers to Freud he also emphasizes that sublimation is a change without repression.[4] It is, as I have said, not particularly clear whether Freud imposes one or two conditions regarding the change that occurs on the side of the object-pole. Does the qualification of 'social valuation' suffice for what is meant by the change of object, or does this change mean something else? Is social valuation something added to a change of object, or does the change fall together with what Freud understands by social valuation? In short, is a real change of object required to take place alongside, and somewhat independent of, social valuation?

1. Is a change of object a necessary precondition for sublimation?

It is well known that, for Freud, only the sexual instincts are susceptible to sublimation. According to Freud, from the fact that the ego-instincts are incapable of being sublimated one could infer that a change of object, or at least the possibility of a change, is a necessary condition for sublimation. Ego-instincts cannot be sublimated because both their aim and their object *are not plastic enough*. The comparison with the ego-instincts in fact carries a new problem along with it. Namely, it is quite clear what is and what is not possible with the object of the ego-instincts. Their objects can only vary within the boundaries of a single species: the object must be edible or drinkable, which is to say, nourishing. It is true that there are more meanings associated with eating and drinking than simply satisfying hunger or quenching thirst (for example, the realm of eating habits, the importance of the person with whom one dines or from whom a child receives food, the memories that go along with it, etc.). Yet regardless how important they may

---

[3] Jacques Lacan, *The Ethics of Psychoanalysis, 1959-1960 : The Seminar of Jacques Lacan, Book VII*, edited by Jacques-Alain Miller, trans. Dennis Porter (London : Tavistock/Routledge, 1992), 293/2. References to this text indicated by page number/paragraph.

[4] J. Lacan, *The Ethics of Psychoanalysis*, 293/3.

be, these additional meanings do not determine the nutritional value of food. Being-nutritious is, strictly speaking, an objective quality. Well then, perversions demonstrate that the variability of the objects of the sexual instincts is exceptionally broader than that of the ego-instincts. The sexual drives may equally well find satisfaction in objects that are not in the least appropriate for reproduction. Sexual instincts are only interested in the satisfaction of desire, and not in finding an object upon which an action can be taken that is adequate and effective from the perspective of reproduction. The object of the sexual instincts is not circumscribed within a single species. Moreover, being sexual is not a natural quality of objects. The sexual attraction of an object is inextricably bound to its symbolic value. As a result, it is not at all clear what it could mean to exchange a sexual object for a non-sexual object.

Lacan as well was occupied with the question of the '*Wechsel des Objekts*' (change of objects). This is not surprising considering that he, in contrast to Freud, interprets sublimation as a process where, in the first place, something occurs on the side of the object of the drive. "Thus, the most general formula that I can give you of sublimation is the following: it raises an object—and I don't mind the suggestion of a play of words in the term I use—to the dignity of the Thing."[5] It is true that, according to Lacan, the change on the side of the object must have repercussions on the side of the aim. According to Lacan, this change consists in a revelation of something that has to do with the true nature of the drive. Revelation is not the change that Freud had in mind when he defined sublimation as a turning away from the original sexual aim. "The sublimation that provides the *Trieb* with a satisfaction different from its aim ... is precisely that which reveals the true nature of the *Trieb* insofar as it is not simply instinct, but has a relationship to *das Ding* as such, to the Thing insofar as it is distinct from the object."[6] What is revealed, as we will see shortly, is the fact that the drive, contrary to the instincts, is in relation with a peculiar object that is not really an object, an object Lacan calls *la Chose*. For Freud, sublimation need not create any insight regarding an unconscious truth. It is a *transformation* of the partial drives. That is to say, it transforms the perverse components of the sexual instincts.[7] One who sublimates neither has to know nor physically feel which instincts are internally transformed. That sublimation is something other than repression means for Lacan that sublimation goes together with a move from non-knowing to knowing, which is to say, with a partial victory over repression.[8] Sublimation provides desire

5   Ibid., 112/1.
6   Ibid., 111/7.
7   Freud, "'Civilized' Sexual Ethics and the Modern Nervous Illness", *SE IX*, 189. "The forces that can be employed for cultural activities are thus for a great extent obtained through the suppression of what are known as the *perverse* elements of sexual excitation."
8   J. Lacan, *The Ethics of Psychoanalysis*, 293/5.

with a new insight into its own truth. It is important to keep in mind that for Lacan, the question of the 'Wechsel des Objekts' does not concern la Chose, but rather the object that brings desire into contact with la Chose.

To answer the question, "What happens to the object of the instinct in sublimation?", Lacan takes a short detour ending in the enigmatic formula, "a change of the object in itself."[9] Lacan first asks—and this is the detour—about the conditions of possibility for the change. "If the drive allows the change of the object, it is because it is already deeply marked by the articulation of the signifier."[10] What does this mean? If a person excites you, or if you desire someone, you cannot describe with great precision what in the person attracts you. You may indeed be able to more or less localize the force of attraction, but are unable to express what is so fascinating about it. Attraction is loosely connected with associative ties that float around and resonate within the object desired. These associations constitute the *signifying-character* of an object, and also serve to direct desire toward other objects. What sets desire in motion is the strained relation between an object and its symbolic value. The *signifying-character* of an object explains why the object is exchangeable. With this, the question of whether the 'Wechsel des Objekts' is necessary remains unanswered.

Now it cannot be the case that sublimation is nothing else than the insertion or creation of a new sign-object (*signifier*) that is either added to the already available signs or takes their place. If this were the case, then sublimation would do nothing else than keep the machinery of desire in motion. While sublimation cannot be called a success if it suffocates desire, the essence of sublimation does not consist in keeping desire in motion. Because a change of object is much too broad a notion, Lacan launches a new formula, "a change of the object in itself." Lacan: "In effect, the rabbit to be conjured from the hat is already to be found in the instinct. This rabbit is not a new object; it is a change of the object in itself."[11] Lacan is saying two things here: one is understandable, the other is bizarre. A magician can only pull a rabbit out of a hat if it is already in his hood or up his sleeve. Likewise, the object that comes forth in sublimation, and directs desire toward la Chose, is already present in the instinct. This much is clear. Then, however, Lacan introduces the bizarre formula, "a change of the object in itself." This expression makes one think of the doctrine of transubstantiation that the church fathers in Trent used to describe the mystery of the Eucharist in order to protect it against the obtrusive curiosity of scientific reason.[12] What type of

9   Ibid., 293/4.
10 Ibid., 293/4. This formula only appears twice in Lacan's seminar: 293/5.
11 Ibid., 293/4.
12 For elaboration, see my "The Sense of Symbols as the Core of Religion," in J. Faulconer, ed., *Transcendence in Philosophy and Religion* (Bloomington: Indiana University Press, 2003), 53-69. Lacan refers to this theological discussion in *Le*

modification does Lacan have in mind here? Has it to do with some sort of transubstantiation of the object, a process as peculiar as the desexualization of the libido, a term that Freud sometimes uses to characterize sublimation and that Lacan, in his treatment of courtly love, ridicules?[13] It cannot be that, by "change of the object in itself," Lacan means the process whereby an object is transformed into a sign of something else. As a characterization of sublimation, this is much too general.

Sublimation does something else than refer desire from one signifier to another signifier. Should sublimation do nothing else, no difference could be established between sublimating and symbolizing. To be sure, sublimating is not possible without symbolizing, but this does not imply that to symbolize is the same as to sublimate.[14] The following suggestion may throw some light on what Lacan possibly means: the intervention of sublimation entails that an object is removed from its familiar environs. The object turns, as it were, on its axis ("a change of the object in itself"), and thereby changes the dynamic of desire. Instead of sprinting ahead and overtaking itself, desire is called to a halt by the object that has been taken out of its familiar context. The object causes a sort of shock, as a result of which desire momentarily holds its breath and folds back upon itself. Desire makes a pirouette; the object turns, as it were, on its axis; and, in that whirlpool, desire obtains some insight into its own dynamic. It is thus important that the ordinary referential process, where desire moves from one signifier to another, is disrupted, and that desire, during the interruption, catches something of *la Chose*.

Let us return briefly to Freud's formulation in his *New Introductory Lectures on Psychoanalysis*. Change is a relative notion. Its content varies according to the initial term against which the change is measured. In order to get a grip on the question of what occurs on the side of the object in sublimation, the problem must be poured into a more precise form. What does sublimation do with the original object of the instinct? I propose that we think of the original object as the object linked to the instinct at the moment sublimation occurs. The question then is as follows: must *this* object be exchanged for another object, or not? Does the transformation of the aim *necessarily* go together with a change of object, or may a sublimated instinct retain the same object? What do Freud and Lacan think about this?

A change of object is in no ways a sufficient condition for authentic sublimation. This is beyond debate. For both Freud and Lacan, replacing an object (a signifier, a woman) with another object (signifier, woman) does not suffice to speak of sublimation. But is replacing the original object, as I

Séminaire de Jacques Lacan: Livre VIII, Le transfert 1960-1961(Paris: Éditions du Seuil, 1991), 290, 302.

[13] J. Lacan, *The Ethics of Psychoanalysis*, 111/4.

[14] Cf. Paul Moyaert, *Begeren en vereren : Idealisering en sublimering* (Nijmegen : SUN, 2002), 75-81.

defined above, a necessary condition? The few indications one can find in Freud regarding this question make one suppose he means that a change of object is necessary. I will argue that it is not a necessary condition. But, for a real understanding of Freud, it is more important to understand why in fact he gave so little attention to this problem. From what Lacan claims regarding the magician's rabbit, I infer that Lacan is rather of the opinion that a change of object is not necessary. But to understand Lacan, one has to see that what he says about the role of the object in sublimation quite radically changes Freud's view of sublimation.

I will use the question regarding the status of the object in the sublimated instinct as a starting point from which to clarify a number of aspects in Freud's and Lacan's view of sublimation. There is a passage in Freud's *Three Essays on the Theory of Sexuality* that is very appropriate to further explore this problematic, and this is the passage where Freud discusses *fetishism*.[15] To be able to explain why fetishism is important, I must first explain how Freud discusses this phenomenon in his *Three Essays on the Theory of Sexuality*, and how this approach relates to his later, more widely known study, "Fetishism."[16]

2. Freud: Perverse and Non-perverse Expressions of Fetishism

Freud's treatment of fetishism in the *Three Essays on the Theory of Sexuality* continues to receive far less attention in psychoanalytic literature than his "Fetishism" article from 1927. One reason for this is that Freud, in the first edition of the *Three Essays on the Theory of Sexuality* from 1905, gave little attention to a psychodynamic explanation of this sexual deviation. He was at first of the opinion that Binet's simple explanation would suffice. This explanation goes approximately as follows: sexual preferences always simply return to the first strong sexual impressions, which originate in early childhood and continue to have an effect on the actual choice of object.[17] While Freud later considered this explanation insufficient, and even rejected it,[18] in my opinion it remains significant. Why? In this explanation, fetishism is neither labeled a defense mechanism, nor a compromise formation between two contradictory tendencies in instinctual life. The emphasis rests on the adhesive force of the first pregnant sexual impressions. The power exerted by fetishistic traits is the pleasure experienced through a certain constellation of impressions. This pleasure has no negative motivation; it is not grounded in avoiding displeasure. It seems that—from the additions to the later, expanded

---

[15] S. Freud, *Three Essays on the Theory of Sexuality*, *SE VII*, 150-55.
[16] S. Freud, "Fetishism", *SE XXI*, 152-7.
[17] S. Freud, *Three Essays on the Theory of Sexuality*, *SE VII*, 154.
[18] Ibid., 154 n. 2, added in 1920 edition.

editions of the *Three Essays on the Theory of Sexuality*—Freud was gradually working on an explanation whose tone pointed toward "Fetishism." The psychodynamic explanation of fetishism as a sexual perversion is more subtle in "Fetishism," but then again, in his study from 1927, Freud no longer considers the possibility that the sexual preference for a woman adorned with a fetish does not necessarily need to be a defense mechanism against, for instance, the fear of the naked body of the woman. In his later study, interest in the fetish rests solely on a negative motivation (the instinct chooses for a fetish out of fear of something else). In his earlier study, it is quite possible that the instinct chooses for a fetish because a person is more attractive and exciting with the fetish than without the fetish. But irrespective of which psychodynamic explanation of fetishism as a sexual deviation is more correct, Freud's discussion in the *Three Essays* still remains very interesting because there he differentiates various forms of fetishism. These distinctions are no longer addressed in "Fetishism." Therein, fetishism is presented as a *phenomenon without variants*. This clarifies why Freud, in his study from 1927, looks for only one model of explanation. On the contrary, in his *Three Essays on the Theory of Sexuality*, Freud is fascinated with the variations of the sexual instincts related to fetishism, variations that, while they participate in normal love, border on the pathological.[19]

Three Essays on the Theory of Sexuality

In *Three Essays on the Theory of Sexuality*, Freud draws a distinction between perversions with respect to the aim (the sexual action), and perversions with respect to the object of the sexual instinct. Now, it goes without saying that fetishism has to be included in the second group of perversions. But Freud does not do this. From the standpoint of classification he recognizes that this is incoherent, and he suggests the following justification: "We have postponed their mention [i.e., cases of fetishism] till we could become acquainted with the factor of sexual overvaluation, on which these phenomena, being connected with an abandonment of the sexual aim, are dependent."[20]

Fetishism *overvalues* an object that is directly or indirectly connected to a normal sexual object—an adult person of the opposite sex. The overvalued object functions as a substitute for the normal sexual object: it takes the place of the normal object, assumes its role and assimilates its sexual significance (only in later editions of the *Three Essays* does Freud unilaterally connect the fetish to the shocking perception of the sexual organs of the woman, and

---

[19] Ibid., 153. "No other variation of the sexual instinct that borders on the pathological can lay so much claim to our interest as this one, such is the particularity of the phenomena to which it gives rise."
[20] Ibid., 153.

conceive the fetish as a screen that more or less hides the lack of the expected male member). The fetish is an *Ersatz* that simultaneously embodies and represents what it replaces.[21] In fetishism as a perversion, the sexual aim is directed toward an inappropriate object. The fetishist prefers masturbation, carried out with his own hands, above sexual intercourse. *Perverse* fetishism is the man's privilege. Of course, it is quite possible that in order to provide a man with sexual pleasure, a woman is prepared to wear a fetish. But one rarely finds a woman who needs a man with a fetish in order to be capable of masturbating, and this because she would prefer masturbation above sexual intercourse. If, on the other hand, one disconnects the interest in fetishistic attributes from the urge of a *perverse* sexual aim, then there is no reason to strictly distinguish, on this level, male and female interests.

Why does Freud need overvaluation in order to explain fetishism? Earlier in *Three Essays on the Theory of Sexuality*, Freud had considered over-valuation as a psychic process explaining the extension and expansion of sexual interests. When in love, sexual overvaluation is not limited to the sexual organs. The sexual instincts gain strength through overvaluation. Sexual interest spontaneously spreads out over the entire body and the libido thereby involves all the sense impressions coming from the sexual object in sexual pleasure. Overvaluation results in an over-eroticizing of the body: parts of the body that are usually not particularly seductive become sexually attractive. The effects of overvaluation, Freud notes, are difficult to reconcile with the idea that the aim of the instinct is naturally limited to the union of the sexual organs.[22] But in fetishism as a sexual perversion, it is not so much a matter of an expansion, but rather a *displacement of sexual interests that ends in a narrowing of these interests*. Sexual interest for a part of the body is *not* reconnected to the sexual interest for the entire body of the person. Rather, the part takes the place of the whole and assumes its significance, resulting in an improper substitution for the sexual object. Sexual overvaluation only explains how fetishism is possible. Freud explains the fixation on the fetish by factors that hinder attainment of the normal sexual aim (for instance, impotence, the price and the risk of the sexual act, unavailability of the normal love object).[23]

---

[21]   The fetish may be a part of the body, a bodily defect, or a lifeless object that has a demonstrable, and preferably sexual, relation to the sexual person who wears it.

[22]   Freud, *Three Essays on the Theory of Sexuality*, 150-1: "The appreciation extends to the whole body of the sexual object and tends to involve every sensation derived from it... . This sexual overvaluation is something that cannot be easily reconciled with a restriction of the sexual aim to union of the actual genitals and it helps to turn activities connected with other parts of the body into sexual aims.

[23]   Ibid.,155-6.

Freud differentiates fetishism as a sexual perversion from fetishistic interests that strictly speaking are not a perversion, and yet do not play an unimportant role in normal love. The various forms of fetishism share a strong interest for a *partial object* (the fetish) that forms a part of a larger whole. What distinguishes them depends on the origin of the fetishistic trait, on its function in sexual desire, and on the relation between part and whole:

> The transition to those cases of fetishism in which the sexual aim, whether normal or perverse, is entirely abandoned is afforded by other cases in which the sexual object is required to fulfill a fetishistic condition—such as the possession of some particular hair-colouring or clothing, or even some bodily defect.[24]

> The point of contact with the normal is provided by the psychologically essential overvaluation of the sexual object, which inevitably extends to everything that is associated with it. A certain degree of fetishism is thus habitually present in normal love, especially in those stages of it in which the normal sexual aim seems unattainable or its fulfillment prevented.[25]

> The situation only becomes pathological when the longing for the fetish passes beyond a point of being merely a necessary condition attached to the sexual object and actually *takes the place* of the normal aim, and, further, when the fetish becomes detached from a particular individual and becomes the *sole* sexual object.[26]

Freud's exposition is not crystal-clear. It is unclear whether or not the cases mentioned in the first citation correspond with those mentioned in the second. But the textual difficulties do not hinder, on the basis of Freud's observations, facile differentiation of at least three forms of fetishism.

As our *starting point* we take Freud's insight that fetishistic interests always play a role in normal love. By this it is meant that overvaluation of the love object (being in love with a person) can awaken sexual interest for partial features associated with the person. It would be incorrect to label this an expression of fetishism. The interest in separate parts of the body does not exist independently and it yields willingly to the striving for the normal sexual aim. Sexual interaction between fetishistic characteristics and the person is integrated by the normal sexual goal.

Fetishistic interests can isolate themselves herein, and more particularly, according to Freud, in phases of love where sexual intercourse cannot be consummated. This is the *first group* of fetishism. Interest in the fetish here

---

[24] Ibid., 153.
[25] Ibid., 153-4.
[26] Ibid., 154.

flows forth from the love for a person, which is not the case in fetishism that is unambiguously perverse. Fetishes from the first group are thus relics as well. A relic has a symbolic surplus value in comparison to objects of similar appearance: this surplus value rests on the fact that the object has belonged to or been touched by the loved, admired, or cherished person. Moreover, a relic is a highly individualized sign-object; a relic is not exchangeable. This expression of fetishism is not perverse: *primo*, because it arises out of love; *secundo*, because it is embedded in a love relation; and *tertio*, because it only temporarily replaces the normal sexual aim and so does not fully embody it. The libido ultimately flows back toward the person to whom the fetish owes its symbolic surplus value. This expression is not perverse even when the abandonment of the sexual aim does not go together with the abandonment of a perverse aim. *I* see no reason why, from a Freudian perspective, this expression of fetishism should not be considered as a *sublimated form of fetishism*. Freud does not do this, despite the fact that he illustrates this group with a striking citation from Goethe's *Faust*:

> Get me a kerchief from her breast,
> A garter that her knee has pressed.[27]

This expression of fetishism could eventually develop into a pious adoration of a person via the worshiping of a relic.[28] Burning a candle on the mantle by the garter of my absent love.

In the *second group*, fetishistic interest is not the result of an unrealizable, reciprocal sexual love, but a constitutive condition for both love and the sexual act. The fetish is not the consequence of overvaluation, but causes overvaluation. The fetish creates the value of the love object and gives a sexual surplus value to the wearer of the fetish. Freud claims that a certain weakening of the normal sexual aim characterizes every case of fetishism.[29] While this claim is not incorrect, it must be added that a fetish can indeed support a wilting sexual urge. The fetish can function as a stimulus that awakens sexual desire, and furthermore, gives it a push in the right direction. In this group the fetish does not function as a defense mechanism, but as a prosthesis or stimulus that can awaken, excite, and support the instinct. The

---

[27]   Ibid.

[28]   It is not clear why Freud does not bring this expression of fetishism into connection with sublimation. One possible explanation is that Freud, although he introduced the term sublimation as a technical term in 1905, was still not really occupied with a theory of sublimation. Another explanation is that Freud placed high demands on the diversion and transformation of the sexual impulses which is required for authentic sublimation.

[29]   Ibid., 153: "Some degree of diminution in the urge towards the normal sexual aim (an executive weakness of the sexual apparatus) seems to be a necessary precondition in every case."

role the fetish here plays corresponds with Lacan's definition of *"l'objet a comme support du désir."* No defense against anxiety, but a means to rouse the sexual drives from their lethargy. Since Freud, and partly under his influence, philosophy relates fetishism to the idea that the person alone, that is to say, the naked body without attributes or the person without signs, generally has little success in animating the libido. Being without shimmering appearance lacks suggestive depth and being without signs does not set the imagination in motion. A garter can really make the libido blossom in a miraculous way. To state this otherwise: a person usually needs the charms of ridiculous and futile fetishistic allures in order to be sexually attractive. Contrary to the first group, these prostheses do not individualize the love object. Indeed, *anyone* prepared to be ornamented with the 'right' fetish, provided a number of additional conditions related to the imaginary *Gestalt* of the body, can ignite someone else's libido. This form of fetishism brings to light the anonymous, impersonal exterior of sexual love. It will, nevertheless, be incorrect to conclude from these anthropological considerations that we are all perverse in the same sense. According to Freud, a fetishistic object choice is not perverse when the libido, supported on a fetishistic interest, proceeds to accomplish the sexual act. Well then, in the second group the fetish fully realizes its signifying value, considering that the libidinal power of the fetish is transferred to the person and guides the libido toward the sexual act.

Fetishism is unequivocally perverse—this is the *third group*—when: *primo*, the desire for the fetish leads its own life outside the circumstances of sexual love for a person (difference with the first group); and, *secundo*, the perverse aim pushes the normal aim from its place (difference with the second group). Characteristic for this perversion is that the fetishistic interest is absolutized and isolated. What does this mean? The perverse fetish is isolated from the broader configuration that it nevertheless needs in order to exert its power of attraction. For regardless how important it may be, the fetish is not attractive of its own accord. It is only attractive in combination with something else, and more specifically, with a person of the opposite sex. The garter needs the link with a person, and, in this sense, the fetish also functions here as a sign. But in unequivocally perverse fetishism, the fetish is a sign that simultaneously blocks and cuts through its own value as a symbol, doing so in approximately the same sense as an obsessive thought, an unrelenting fantasy image, or an oppressive hallucination. The fetish is a *fascinating* object that *blocks the referential function* it nevertheless needs in order to exert its influence. The following characterization, formulated in moral terms, will clarify what I mean.

In perversion the person functions as a sort of appendix to the fetish. The fetishist does not thank the person for the pleasure he nonetheless receives from her via the fetish she wears. And how can you better thank a person in sexual love than by returning the pleasure received, even the pleasure that you received via the fetish? And in what does this reciprocation consist if not in allowing the woman, together with her body, to enjoy along with you the pleasure you receive via the fetish? But neither the fetishist nor his fetish is prepared to share his pleasure with the one who wears the fetish. The fetishist prefers masturbation. He is ungrateful, and his fetish behaves like a greedy object. Avarice is a pathetic vice. The fetish keeps for itself the meaning it has nevertheless received. As opposed to the second group, the fetish yields *no sexual surplus value* to the wearer of the fetish. The fetish isolates itself and closes itself up in its own world, from which the one who wears it is excluded. The wearer of the fetish receives nothing in return for the fetish that she wears. In perverse fetishism, the sexually exciting power of the fetish does not return to the one who wears of the fetish. In this sense, the sign-value of the fetish is blocked.

The Fetish in Perversion and in Sublimation

From the previous discussion, it seems that the fetish in the third group, in distinction from that in the first and second group, does not fully exercise its symbolic value. Now, one may wonder if this difference does not provide an interesting indication for distinguishing how *the fetish*, that is to say, *a dependent partial object*, functions in perversion and sublimation. What would this difference look like?

In perversion, the fetish monopolizes attention, thereby exerting a *centripetal* and quasi-stultifying force. The perverse fetish absorbs all significance into itself, ultimately resulting in a meaningless object. In sublimation it is just the reverse: the fetish exerts an evocative and thus *centrifugal* significative power. The perverse fetishist degrades the woman because he reduces her to a garter. The artist does just the opposite. He raises the garter to a suggestive sign of the woman and is even able to catch some of her beauty in the garter, without thereby severing the link with the ordinary character of the fetish. The perverse fetishist deprives the woman of her dignity. Art can be a consecration of the ordinary. Or, formulated in Lacan's terminology: art is as a serving-tray on which my ridiculous garter can be presented with some glory. Perversion reduces *la Chose* to a graspable, manipulable object, while sublimation raises the object to a suggestive sign of *la Chose*. The distinction that I have in mind here corresponds with the difference between a fascinating and a poetic object.

Freud, however, can do little with the proposal I have just formulated. In his view, the distinction *centrifugal-centripetal* is incapable of saying anything of real importance regarding the specific role of the object in perversion and sublimation. Why? One may exchange the object, or make as many changes to the object as one likes, but as long as the aim of the instinct is not altered there can be no talk of sublimation. On this point Freud does nothing but repeat what we already knew: one can say nothing significant about sublimation by analyzing only what happens with the object of the drive. Otherwise formulated: even if it is not necessary to exchange the object (against Freud), then we are only correct regarding one point that, according to Freud, is totally irrelevant for the distinction between perversion and sublimation. This is not to exclude the possibility, however, that the distinction centrifugal-centripetal, *combined* with other criteria, can indeed be relevant.

Fetishism

In *Fetishism*, Freud no longer conceives the fetish as a substitute for the sexual person. The fetish is now an *Ersatz* for what incarnates the being-sexed of the woman, which is to say the female genital. Freud no longer connects the fetish in any way to the inaccessibility of the beloved, as is the case, for instance, in the first group from the *Three Essays on the Theory of Sexuality*. For the fetishist, the fetish functions solely as protection against anxiety, and more specifically, against the anxiety for an imaginary castration that can be executed on his body. The perception of the female genital always again feeds his phantasm of imaginary castration. The fetish *in some sense* still *seems* to fill the role of a symbol, at least in the sense that a symbol in one and the same movement lets something appear and withdraws it from view. The fetish *seems* to be *a sort of symbol*, at least insofar as one takes the veil as a prototype for symbols. If the fetish would, in its characteristically ambiguous manner, let appear what it hides, it should in principle make no difference if one who wears the fetish is a man or a woman. But this is not the case. There may be no doubt for the fetishist regarding the sexual identity of the person who wears the fetish. The fetish must remain in the fetishist's field of vision, for he does not want to be deceived. Neither the disappearance of sexual difference, nor the disappearance of the signs that reveal and support sexual difference, are a source of sexual excitation. The idea that the woman is not a woman, but could be a man dressed as a woman, is not in the least exciting for the fetishist. The fetish erects a dam against the female genital, whose direct sight *impresses and inspires anxiety* in the fetishist. This reaction is, I think, not radically different from the reaction that, for instance, the apparition of the Lady in courtly love provokes in the troubadour. The fetish functions as a screen that hinders the free radiance of the naked body of the woman: it must divert attention from what it must nevertheless allow to shine through.

But it is too simple to reduce his anxiety, which in no way spoils his sexual pleasure, to anxiety for the perception of the female genital. No, what causes his anxiety is losing sight of the female genital. For the fetishist, sexual difference remains associated with the confused idea that this difference was not always there, and thus could once again disappear. He understands sexual difference in terms of a lack that could just as well not have been there. To put it in Lacan's vocabulary: the imaginary interpretation of sexual difference disrupts the symbolic interpretation of this difference. Well then, the fetish must not only cover what he, the fetishist, understands as a deficiency. The fetish must as well guarantee him that something is not there. It must assure him that sexual difference, whose existence he mistrusts, nevertheless persists. If one understands, as Lacan does, the phallus as symbol of sexual difference that conveys its meaning to different bodily signs thanks to its anatomical anchoring, then the fetish fulfils the role of a supplementary symbol. That is to say, it fulfils the role of a prosthesis that must support the vacillating symbolic value of the phallus. The fetish partly assumes the task of the phallus which inadequately performs its symbolic function.

On the one hand, fetishism as a sexual deviation only relates to signs that can be separated from the real object (the sexual person who wears the fetish), without the sexual identity of the wearer thereby being changed. Appearance (that is to say, exterior signs that both veil castration and allow it to appear) and essence (that is to say, the sexual identity of the wearer of the fetish) are not confused with one another. The fetishist actually believes in what he only indirectly perceives—in other words, he believes that she is a woman—and does not believe what he really sees—that is to say, he does not believe she has a phallus. Freud calls this double gesture of belief and disbelief, justifiably compared by Mannoni[30] to the attitude of children with respect to Santa Claus, *Verleugnung. On the other hand*, the fetishist disbelieves his perception. The fact that he knows, and can also see, that the person is really a woman does not suffice to reassure him that she is a woman. The fetish must, as I have said, not only hide the lack. Rather, via the fetish, he makes certain that she is a woman. The fetish gives him this certainty. In opposition to those whose perception is not destabilized by their fantasy world, the fetishist needs at least one prosthetic support to orient and trust his perception. *Verleugnung* testifies to a vacillating belief in perception. This partially explains why Freud in *Fetishism* relates perverse fetishism to the loss of reality in psychosis. Otherwise than in psychosis, it is in fact the case that fetishism: *primo*, has enough with one incidental sign (a fetish) to stabilize the shaky relation *in sexualibus* between appearance and essence, and; *secundo*, that this unsteady relation is enclosed, and thus does not overflow his entire psychical life.

My suggestion, however, that the fetish functions more or less as a sort of symbol is actually misleading. Or, more correctly, it is wrong to compare a fetish with a veil.

> The fetish would therefore *never be a symbol*, but rather like a set and fixed plan, an arrested image, a photo to which one always returns in order to avert the unwelcome sequences of movement, the unfortunate discoveries of an

---

[30] Octave Mannoni, "Je sais bien, mais quand meme", in *Clefs pour l'imaginaire* (Paris: Ed. du Seuil, 1968), 14-5.

exploration: it would represent the last moment where one could still believe (in it).[31]

A veil arouses curiosity. It does not draw attention to itself, but to what it allows to shine through. A veil does not kill the spirit, but is suggestive. In perversion, the fetish functions as a blinding object without any poetic depth: it hinders desire from turning around something other than the fetish, and hinders desire from turning around the fetish. The perverse fetishist rotates with his body solely around his own phallus.

3. Lacan: Sublimation and the Power of the Object

Sublimation for Freud is a psychical process that transforms the aim of the instinct. This transformation goes together with a change of object. For Lacan, sublimation is a process that does something with the object of the instinct, and what occurs with the object causes a change in the dynamic of desire.[32] I recall Lacan's definition: "Thus, the most general formula that I can give you of sublimation is the following: it raises an object…to the dignity of the Thing."[33] Sublimation consists in an elevation of the object. What does Lacan mean by this? Through elevation, the object receives, according to Lacan, something of the *dignity* of *the Thing*. What must one understand by dignity, and what is meant by *la Chose*? To answer these questions, I make a detour via courtly love, Lacan's favorite example[34] of sublimation.

Courtly Love

Courtly love rests on the troubadour's adoration and glorification of the inaccessible and above all unapproachable Lady. In the presence of the troubadour, the Lady assumes the position of a figure ruling over his desires and dominating his instincts. She exudes a power that can force him to his knees and keep his desires at a distance. Her imposing appearance is able to obstruct the spontaneous course of his desires. She finds herself in an elevated

---

[31] Gilles Deleuze, *Présentation de Sacher-Masoch*, (Paris : Ed. de Minuit, Coll. 'Arguments 32, 1967), 29, emphasis added.

[32] One can relate Lacan to Freud as follows. For Freud, it is a crucial question how the transformation from sexual to non-sexual occurs. He has presented two hypotheses for this question. Sublimation can occur via reaction formation and/or via the narcissism of the libido. Concerning what Lacan says regarding courtly love, one may develop the hypothesis that sublimation may also come about via an idealizing of the object. See my *Begeren en vereren: Idealisering en sublimering* (Nijmegen: SUN, 2003), 86-90.

[33] Lacan, *The Ethics of Psychoanalysis, op.cit.*, 112/1.

[34] Ibid., 128/3.

position from where she, like the sovereign God of a voluntaristic theology, rules over his desires. She sits enthroned over the desires of the troubadour; or more accurately, she rises above his desires that she simultaneously awakens. Her presence can inhibit the spontaneous development of the instincts normally directed by the pleasure principle. The effect of her impressive presence on the instincts consists in a pushing up of the sexual instincts, that is to say, their simultaneous arousal and restraint. Now, a figure such as the Lady is only capable of doing this because she can surreptitiously or implicitly exploit instincts that, in their previous history, have developed sensitivity for figures in a comparable position of power. Thus the Lady may undoubtedly profit from, for instance, masochistic trends of the sexual instincts.

Courtly love is neither naturalistic nor platonic. It is too ascetic to be purely corporeal, and too corporeal to dissipate into a spiritual *Schwärmerei*. Although on a bodily level courtly love wants to be a virginal love, it has little in common with a lofty and pure desire of the heart. Sexual satisfaction denied to the instincts will sometimes be articulated, unvarnished, in poems. From this it follows that one cannot speak about courtly love in terms of a repression of the instincts. It is not only that the Lady rises above his desires; at the same time it is the means for the troubadour to surpass his own desires. In short, the elevation of the love object brings the desires of the troubadour to a point of *exaltation*. Well then, transport (ecstasy) is known from way back as one of the important consequences of certain works of art. It would be incorrect to simply describe ecstasy as a transformation of a sexual aim into a non-sexual aim. The demands Freud places on true sublimation are, strictly speaking, much too high to regard courtly love—to take just one example—as a successful sublimation. Freud would not, I think, conceive of courtly love as a full expression of sublimation because the sexual desires and the perverse aspects of sexuality are too emphatically present in it.

Elevation, in the sense of rising up above someone's desires, suggests indifference to the desires one rises above. Because of this indifference, which resonates in her imposing loftiness, the Lady also resembles a figure that is cruel and merciless. She radiates something of the supreme heights of the starry sky above us, which is unmoved by our tears of joy, or by our sorrow. Lacan alludes to this cruelty:

> The Lady is basically what was later to be called, with a childish echo of the original ideology, 'cruel as the tigers of Ircania'. But you will not find the extreme arbitrariness of the attitude expressed any better than among the authors of the period themselves, Chrétian de Troyes, for example.[35]

---

[35]   Lacan, *The Ethics of Psychoanalysis*, 150/8-151.

Lacan says that the Lady is unattainable.[36] "Unattainable" here not only means that the troubadour's desire finds no satisfaction in the Lady, but also that the Lady is inapproachable. The troubadour's hymns and pleads do not reach her, in the sense that they cannot touch her. More correctly formulated, despite her response to his courtship, she remains unmoved, is not touched or stirred by it. She rises above the desires that she simultaneously mobilizes in him. This indifference turns her into an image derived from *la Chose*. But more about this later.

Sublimation through overvaluation of the object

One can understand Lacan's view of transformation in sublimation by the model of a non-traumatic experience of shock. The instincts are surprised and struck by an object that makes an impression on them, and this is because its unusual and surprising presentation is capable of bringing desire to a halt. During the pause or stoppage, the object introduces a new perspective into instinctual life. Sublimation is thus a process that begins with the object, and gives the object the power to put the brakes on the instinct and bring it to insight.[37] The object is displaced from its familiar environment and now rules over its new terrain. The process I am describing here resembles the attitude of '*Achtung*' that, according to Kant, can be brought about by the trans-phenomenological appearance of the categorical imperative; it is also comparable to the feeling of awe and respect with which the visage of the other can fill me; and it seems, finally, like the reserved stance I take when in physical proximity to a dead body. These reactions are a response to the power emanating from the object-pole. However, it must be mentioned that unique to courtly love is how the attitudes of esteem, worship and adoration are provoked by the sensual perfections of the love object. Otherwise than in apparently similar practices of worship in the Roman religion, the worship of the Lady is not borne by the ideal image of moral perfection. The Lady is no saint.

Lacan calls the process by which an object gains power, and thereby transcends its own environment, *to raise an object*. This process corresponds to what in psychoanalysis since Freud has been named idealization (overvaluation). Lacan also conceives the idealization of the Lady as the *sublimation of the object*: "what Freud would call *Überschätzung* or overvaluation of the object—and that I will henceforth call object

---

[36] Ibid., 158/3
[37] It is evident that this approach to sublimation is primarily appropriate for art and religion, and not for science. It is understandable that Lacan, otherwise than Freud, estimates the power of sublimation to be higher than, and deems it more important than, that of science.

61

sublimation."[38] In Freud's technical vocabulary, the expression *sublimation of the object* is quite simply absurd. The aim of the instinct can be sublimated, but not the object. Lacan, however, seems to coalesce the idealization of the object and sublimation. From Freud's point of view, he confuses them. In a well known passage from "On Narcissism: An Introduction", Freud describes idealization as *psychische Erhöhung* [mental exaltation].[39]

Let us assume that what Lacan means with *raising* agrees with what Freud understands by the idealization of the object. Well then, in the familiar passage from "On Narcissism", to which I just alluded, Freud says that it is important not to confuse idealization and sublimation with one another:

> We are naturally led to examine the relation between this forming of an ideal and sublimation. Sublimation is a process that concerns object-libido and consists in the instinct's directing itself towards an aim other than and remote from, that of sexual satisfaction; in this process the accent falls upon deflection from sexuality. Idealization is a process that concerns the *object*; by it that object, without any alteration in its nature, is aggrandized and exalted in the subject's mind. Idealization is possible in the sphere of ego-libido as well as in that of object-libido. For example, the sexual overvaluation of an object is an idealization of it. In so far as sublimation describes something that has to do with the instinct and idealization something to do with the object, the two concepts are to be distinguished from each other.[40]

Freud expresses himself rather clumsily in this passage for two reasons. He suggests that only the self and the independent (the person) or dependent object of the drive (the fetish, for example) may be the object of idealization. In *Three Essays on the Theory of Sexuality*, Freud says that the instinct can also be idealized.[41] Furthermore, he suggests that idealization of the object, contrary to sublimation, exerts no influence on the instinct, which is to say that it has no influence on the aim of the instinct. However, this is not the case. It generally follows from falling in love (that is to say, the idealization of a person) that the instincts are aroused and increase in strength. Idealization of the object is not without consequences for the instinct. Freud intends to say that idealization neither reorients the aim of the instinct, nor transforms it. The nature of the interest remains unchanged. And this is specifically how idealization is distinguished from sublimation. But what is idealized does indeed increase in strength. Idealization exerts pressure on the instinct, and influences what Freud has called the *pressure* (*'Drang'*) of the instinct. *This*

---

[38] Lacan, *The Ethics of Psychoanalysis*, 109/2. See also, 112/2: "the sublimation of the feminine."

[39] Freud, 'Zur Einfürung des Narzissmus', *Gesammelte Werke, X*, 161: "Die Idealisierung ist ein Vorgang mit dem Objekt, durch welchen dieses ... psychisch erhöht wird."

[40] Freud, "On Narcissism: An Introduction", *SE XIV*, 94.

[41] Freud, *Three Essays on the Theory of Sexuality*, 161.

62

modification is solely a question of increasing and decreasing the amount of libidinal cathexes. In short: in contrast to sublimation, idealization only results in a *gradual* modification of instinctual tension.

Freud thus draws a sharp distinction between idealization and sublimation. Still, Lacan describes courtly love as the *sublimation de l'objet*. Is this conceptual sloppiness, even a confused understanding? Or does Lacan, with this expression, want to suggest that a direct causal relation exists, or may exist, between both processes? In my concise presentation of courtly love, I have strongly emphasized the aspect of rapture. Lacan does not use this term. But this term, in my judgment, once again makes clear the direct connection between idealization and sublimation. Rapture is the intersection of the two processes, and may thus illuminate Lacan's motivation for approaching sublimation from the perspective of courtly love. Exaltation originates from the clash of two mutually opposed streams of feeling. Exaltation is the intersection of two processes that can simultaneously spring from the idealization of the love object and, more specifically, from an excessive idealization. These two streams are: stimulation and inhibition of the sensual instincts. The confrontation between these two streams of feeling, where inhibition has the upper hand, results in a pushing up or an exaltation of the sensual instincts. Exaltation may eventually develop into adoration and worship. And what is courtly love if not a cultivation of such adoration? What is it if not a cult of the Lady who, elevated as she is, rises above the desires that she sets in motion (intensification, stirring up of desires), and who, because of her inaccessible elevation, at the same time defies (inhibits) these desires?

My interpretation of Lacan's favorite example seems to contain elements incompatible with some fundamental Freudian insights. I stated above that, proceeding from "On Narcissism: An Introduction", the development of the idealization of the instincts runs in a straight line. Idealization only results in an increase of strength, and it increases the power of the instinct. To put this in Freud's economical perspective, the only thing that occurs is a redistribution of the available amount of energy. Yet even with Freud matters are not that simple. For, Freud as well gives indications that suggest that the influence of object idealization upon the instincts is less straightforward. Which indications?[42] Freud connects the idealization of the love object with the formation of what he calls *aim-inhibited* instincts. At first sight, one would be able to bring *aim-inhibited* into connection with exaltation, were it not that Freud intends with this term a rather specific vicissitude of the instincts. He conceives *aim-inhibited* as a softening and weakening of the sensual instincts; stated otherwise, *aim-inhibited* instincts are tender instincts. If rapture has anything to do with the hindrance of the instincts, then one cannot describe

---

[42] For a systematic discussion of the effects of idealization on instinctual life: Moyaert, *Begeren en Vereren: Idealisering en sublimering*, 86-126.

this inhibition as a weakening and softening of sensual cravings. But Freud does not limit the inhibitive effects of object-idealization to the formation of tender expressions of instinct.

In chapter VII of his *Group Psychology and the Analysis of the Ego*,[43] "Being in Love and Hypnosis", Freud notes still other effects that equally bear witness to an inhibitive effect of object-idealization. The idealization of the object may *separate* sensual and non-sensual instinctual expressions; it may *suppress* the sensual expressions of instinct (Freud uses '*unterdrücken*', sloppily translated in the *Standard Edition* as *being repressed*), it may *set them aside* ('*Zurücksetzung der sinnlichen Strebungen*') or *push them into the background* ('*zurück gedrangt werden*'). According to my interpretation of courtly love, idealization of the object can also bring the instincts into transport. Rapture actually expresses itself as a damming up of instincts and it is, phenomenologically-speaking, wrong to describe this elaboration merely as repression. However, the fact that Freud, in chapter VII of *Group Psychology and the Analysis of the Ego*, uses different terms to describe the inhibitive effect of object idealization shows that he is not prepared to simply identify this inhibition with repression. Allow me to formulate it otherwise: idealization of the object *may* mobilize repression, but it does not necessarily do so. Inspired by Lacan's example, one may redefine sublimation as the inhibition[44] of instinct without repression.

Now that I have made it plausible that idealization and sublimation may be very closely related, I must explain what Lacan means by *la Chose* and *la dignité*.

The Elevation of "la Chose"

It is known that Lacan found the term *das Ding* in a short passage from *Entwurf einer Psychologie* (*Project for a Scientific Psychology*), where Freud said something about what he called the complex of the *Nebenmensch*, a complex that thereafter no longer appeared in Freud's *oeuvre*.[45] What did Lacan see in this?

The child can locate and understand different aspects of the other (for example, the mother). 'Understand' here means recognizing perceptions and bringing them into association with other perceptions already familiar to the child: memory-images, for example, or perceptions of its own body. In this manner, representational complexes originating in the other are taken up into the child's subjective world of representations and affects. Representations

---

[43] Freud, *Group Psychology and the Analysis of the Ego, SE XVIII*, 111-3.

[44] "Aim-inhibited" is not appropriate because this term, according to Freud, generally points to the attenuating of the sensual instincts.

[45] Lacan, *The Ethics of Psychoanalysis*, 38-41.

familiar to the child form the basis of the child's orientation within the entirety of perceptions that come toward it. Woven into these perceptions, other perceptions also appear—such as certain facial expressions—that the child cannot connect to the contents of its own consciousness. The child does not recognize these perceptions, and therefore does not understand them. The familiar is embedded in, and penetrated by, what strikes one as strange. If what is strange in the other moves into the foreground, it can—depending on the manner in which it appears—put the familiar points of orientation under pressure and confuse them. Freud calls what is not understood in the other *das Ding*. What can Lacan do with this?

What Lacan understands by *la Chose* is closely tied to the subjective experience of a loss, or to the failure of a reassuring satisfaction expected from the side of the other to occur. Because this satisfaction does not arrive, the other becomes marked with the confusing characteristics of a cruel and malignant being. The moment desire is contradicted and the expected satisfaction does not directly arrive, all sorts of hostile-intentioned beings come to life in the imagination. The existence of *la Chose* is linked to the perception of a split or division in the attitude toward the other, and more broadly with the perception of a conflictive tension in the relation to the surrounding world and to the cosmos. By 'split' I mean the following: on the one side, perceptions come from the other, which makes it seem that the other is interested in me, goes along with my interests, and accommodates to my desires; but at the same time, signals trickle inside that seem to indicate that the other is turned in on itself and is not interested in me. Where something appears in the other, giving the impression that the other, despite his or her involvement, is indifferent to me, there *das Ding* comes to life. The origination of *la Chose*, as well as its resurrection, is thus associated with negative experiences. The Thing originates and breeds in the interval between my expectations and the reality contradicting my expectations. The manifestation of *la Chose* is rather confusing and bewildering because it puts the reliable points of reference and distinctions on shaky ground. Reality has something double about it, and thus something unreliable and unpredictable. Harpo Marx is a pointed illustration of this duality that turns the other into something incomprehensible. Of the silent Marx who wanders around in the Marx brother's films with a petrified and unfathomable smile, Lacan states:

> It is enough to evoke a face which is familiar to every one of you, that of the terrible dumb brother of the four Marx brothers, Harpo. Is there anything that poses a question which is more present, more pressing, more absorbing, more disruptive, more nauseating, more calculated to thrust everything that takes place before us into the abyss or void than that face of Harpo Marx, that face with its smile which leaves us unclear as to whether it signifies the most extreme perversity or complete simplicity? This dumb man alone is sufficient to sustain the atmosphere of doubt and of radical annihilation which is the stuff

of the Marx brother's extraordinary farce and the uninterrupted play of 'jokes' that makes their activity so valuable.[46]

Harpo Marx is an ambivalent being, a fabricated image of the Thing in the other, or of the other as Thing. But God can also become an artificial image of the Thing. Such is the case, for instance, when He appears in a silent, majestic shroud within a religious context, or when He only lets Himself be recognized as a God who cares nothing for the joys and sufferings of humankind.

In my opinion, the most difficult term to explain in Lacan's definition of sublimation is *dignité*. Dignity can point to the admirable moral attitude of a person who conducts oneself with serenity in times of prosperity or adversity. A person who knows how to act with dignity is not manifestly at the mercy of his emotions and is unmoved by events that overcome him. Dignity bears witness to a certain distancing from involvement, or to transcending the pressure of sensual desires; it evokes a state of exemption from the reactions that an occurrence normally provokes. Dignity is thus an expression of sublimity. A person who behaves with dignity has something untouchable about her, setting her somewhat apart from the circuit of normal, interpersonal relations. I think the idea of distance is central to *dignité*, and this idea is easily associated with the elevation characteristic of the noblewoman adored in courtly love. Well then, both respect and elevation have a double bottom, because in both there is also a certain immovable indifference reverberating within unmoved equanimity. One may hear in it the echo of an indifference that can change into cruelty. Cruel, because the person is no longer moved by what touches other people.

One who bears one's sorrow with dignity remains externally unmoved by adversity. We admire someone who behaves with dignity, but at the same time, dignity can have its terrifying aspects. We admire the conjunction of serenity and involvement; we are frightened by the reversal of elevation into cruel indifference, where maliciousness floats to the surface. A person becomes unapproachable by being admired. But the reverse is also the case: a person compels admiration by his or her inaccessibility. Alongside the Lady in courtly love, Antigone is also an illustration of an elevated attitude where a terribly cold and terrifying indifference with regard to the usual affairs of life is nearly on the point of surfacing. The *philia* calls Antigone, in defiance of Creon's edict, to bury her brother. The deep obligations that blood relations can involve make her transcend the ordinary functioning of the Freudian pleasure principle. What thus clothes her with dignity is the fact that she obeys something stronger than the interests of pleasure and displeasure. But this dignity is, at the same time, suffused with cruelty against Ismene, against Haimon, and also against herself. Antigone takes a unique position insofar as she withdraws herself from the circle of persons that surround her, thereby at

[46]   Ibid., 55/3.

the same time keeping these people at a distance. That we do not perceive her cruel distantiation as repulsive and reprehensible has to do with the fact that Antigone, in her melancholy-saturated lamentation, reflects on all she will miss.

The double bottom of *dignité* fits perfectly with a figure like the Lady who occupies the place of *la Chose* in courtly love. Her sovereignty with respect to the troubadour is also a form of protection against the underlying sadistic cruelty that resides within her, cruelty that she projects. This protection is necessary if one is not to be absorbed and crippled by what comes to the surface in her exaltation. One may see in the Lady the projection of an impossible fulfillment of desire, but one may also see in her the resurrection of a cruel being. There is something to be said for both interpretations, and actually, they do not exclude one another. For, in both cases, desire is confronted with an undermining of its expectations. In this sense, one may see in the lady a sort of reanimation of the Mother.[47] It is still the case, however, that manifestations of a negative ontology (the manifestation of the Thing as the revelation of the fact that something is not there) are less evocative to the imagination than visions in which malicious beings rule over human desires. But the strongest catalyst for the imagination is the unexpected reversal of an ideal into its radical opposite. The unpredictable character of this reversal always again feeds desire with images of an unreliable universe. The death of God does not stimulate the imagination. An unreliable and capricious God speaks louder to fantasy.

I summarize. Sublimation consists in elevating an object above its ordinary value. The raised object is invested with dignity, a term I understand as a synonym for the transcendence of the object with respect to its ordinary value. Dignity has an unmistakably Kantian tenor, but the scope of this term has to be broadened because the object can also be elevated above, and withdrawn from, its moral value. The object isolated by overvaluation gains power: it attracts our desire and at the same time keeps it at a distance. The idealization of the object makes it an appropriate receptacle for the apparition of *la Chose*. I have explained this apparition as potentially destructive of the meanings (*i.e.*, the chain of signifiers) that organize the world in which we live and give it a human face. The unapproachable and unmoved figure of the lady is one striking illustration of a sublime transcendency to whom desire can be submitted and who can hardly hide its cold and indifferent character. The negative repercussions connected with the eruption of *la Chose* may also be revealed in objects that evoke the sudden transition from a human world to an animal world, from the formed to the formless, from the personal to the impersonal, from good to bad.

---

[47]   Ibid., 70/3.

Partial objects can also become objects of overvaluation. Lacan offers some striking examples of sublimation where idealization concerns partial objects, fragments in place of the whole. I limit myself[48] to an incident Lacan had in London, told by way of introduction to his considerations about the painting, "Shoes", by Van Gogh.[49]

Lacan was once in London, where he was lodging in a sort of *Home*. One evening his wife said: "Professor D... is here." This was one of his distinguished professors at the *Ecole des Langues Orientales*. Lacan asked her how she knew, and she answered, "I've seen his shoes." Lacan: "I must say that I couldn't help feeling startled by that answer; I was also sceptical." Why? The personality of such an exceptional individual certainly can't be localized in a pair of nondescript shoes. "I found the thing quite funny and didn't attach any importance to it." Lacan moved further down the hallway and, to his great astonishment, saw *professor D* emerging from his room. The point of this anecdote is the following: we would like our personality to be associated with a work that is valuable, one that carries our personal seal. We would appreciate if people could recognize who we are through our works alone. Now, what appears in Lacan's anecdote? A personality upon whom Lacan thinks back with awe is recognizable by a ridiculous *detail* that is irrelevant to the image he has of the person. The shoes singularize *professor D*, even though they actually say nothing about his great personality. They singularize without definition.

> To read the highly personal traits of an individuality into a pair of clodhoppers sitting outside a door didn't seem to me to be sufficiently convincing evidence, and there was nothing else that allowed me to believe that *Professor D* might be in London.

The shoes suddenly receive a shine (that is to say, overvaluation) for Lacan, by which they speak to him, bring him into slight confusion, and emotionally move him. The shoes do not bring Lacan into transport. The shoes function as a striking sign of a link between the personality and an anonymous exterior; the detail is a turning point between the personal and the impersonal. In this sense, they are a manifestation of *la Chose*. "I find that experience highly instructive, and it is on that basis that I intend to suggest to you the notion of the beautiful." As in the installations of contemporary art, an unexpected

---

[48] For another example, see my comment on Lacan's autobiographical sardine can ; "Sur la sublimation chez Lacan", in *La pensée de Jacques Lacan: Questions historiques-problèmes théoriques*, ed. P. Moyaert and S. Lofts (Leuven-Paris: Editions Peeters, 1994), Collection "Bibliothèque philosophique de Louvain", vol. 39, 125-46.

[49] Lacan, *The Ethics of Psychoanalysis*, 296-7.

configuration gives the shoes a luster that makes them stick out above their use value and above the normal understanding that we have of them.

> You must imagine Professor D…'s clodhoppers *ohne Begriff*, with no thought of the academic, without any connection to his endearing personality, if you are to begin to see Van Gogh's own clodhoppers come alive with their own incommensurable quality of beauty.

The moment they receive a higher rank, the shoes become a sign cut loose from their common significative ties, subsequently returning to us as shoes that evoke the disappearance of all human meaning. In the vulnerable shoes, one catches a glimpse of a more deeply embedded human helplessness, the echo of a cold and indifferent universe. The desolate shoes are a pregnant sign of human abandonment, of our aimlessness in the world, and thus of the collapse of all meaning. Trash then, with a dull shine that speaks to the imagination.

> This signifier [i.e., the shoes] is not even a signifier of walking, of fatigue, or of anything else, such as passion or human warmth. It is just a signifier of that which is signified by a pair of abandoned clodhoppers, namely, both a presence and a pure absence—something that is, if one likes, inert, available to everyone.

Lacan's evocative description of the shoes corresponds to his description of Oedipus in *Séminaire II*: "That is what *Oedipus at Colonus* shows us—the essential drama of destiny, the total absence of charity, of fraternity, of anything whatsoever relating to what one calls human feeling."[50] "As everything right from the start of the tragedy goes to show, Oedipus is nothing more than the scum of the earth, the refuse, the residue, a thing empty of any plausible appearance."[51]

I have suggested that we interpret Lacan's idea of "elevating an object" as an idealization of the object. This interpretation only makes sense if idealization does not necessarily mean the attribution of all sorts of perfections to someone or something. I have distinguished two types of sublimation: the elevation of a person (courtly love); and the elevation of a fetish (clodhoppers). In the example of courtly love, idealization functions as a description and an explanation of sublimation. A description because it clarifies what sublimation is; an explanation because it suggests both how object idealization can indeed transform sexual desire, and why this transformation need not be a radical desexualization. Idealization has

[50] Lacan, *The Ego in Freud's Theory and in the Technique of Psychoanalysis (1954-1955): The Seminar of Jacques Lacan, Book II*, trans. Sylvana Tomaselli (Cambridge: Cambridge University Press, 1988), 230.
[51] Ibid., 232.

explanatory value because the transformative power of the object may be compared with the shock-effect of something that impresses itself on our desires. In cases where a partial object (fetish) is idealized, idealization seems mainly to offer a redescription of what sublimation is and what it does with our desires. It does not explain how it produces this transformation. It is important to emphasize that the sublime elevation of a fetish transforms the role of the perverse fetish. The sublimated fetish no longer functions as a protection against castration anxiety. Perverse fetishism destroys the sign-value of the fetish. Sublimation breathes a poetic life into it.

VERTIGO OF SUBSTITUTES: FETISH AND TROPHY

Jean-Joseph Goux

When Freud referred to fetishism, he was not introducing some novel notion fashioned from within the peculiar theoretical context of psychoanalysis. The notion of fetishism was already present in the vocabulary of psychopathology. Charcot, Binet, and Krafft-Ebing had made detailed descriptions—under the name of fetishism—of numerous cases of this so-called sexual perversion. As Freud refers to these authors, he accepts their denomination as such. From this point of view, Freud is not in the same situation as Marx. The latter, pursuing his singular path, proceeded to draw an analogy with religious fetishism, establishing a new application of the notion in the realm of economic value theory, and thereby creating a new concept of fetishism. Freud does not need to perform the same operation, fetishism already having been recognized as a sexual aberration—generally masculine and rare to find in its pure form—that substitutes an inanimate thing for a so-called normal sexual object, that is to say, for a person of the female gender. This substitute is in some way related to her: a shoe, a garment of lingerie, a laced–up corset, a lock of hair, etc… Sexual satisfaction can only be obtained through *this* object, upon which the entire strength of desire seems to be concentrated. Not only does Freud accept the noseographic picture that establishes the boundary of this easily identifiable aberration; he also assumes the term that designates it as well.

The term "fetishism" has been charged with meanings by ethnology and the history of religions since the work of President de Brosses in the 18th century. The sexual object becomes comparable to one of those fetishes that, as we are told, the savages adore when turning their objects into gods. Freud's contribution does not reside in this analogy between the religious and the sexual, but in the very explanation he provides for the mechanism of the fetishist's desire. Freud finds in fetishism not one deviation amongst others, but an extreme case that obliges him to descend into the heart of the profound mechanism of all perversions; that is, into their relation to the terror of castration, to the ego, and to the law.

1. Binet and Freud

Alfred Binet was the first to analyse sexual fetishism in a detailed and perspicacious way. In 1887 he published a long article in *La revue de philo-sophie* (which is quite illustrative of the interest in psychology in that era), entitled "Le fétichisme dans l'amour".[1] Binet demonstrates the similarities between religious fetishism and fetishism in love from the outset, thus legitimizing the transfer of the original sense of the term from one domain to another. In this respect, it is remarkable that, in the first paragraph of this long article, one reads the astonishing proclamation:

> The great quarrel of images that were agitated from the first century of the Christian era, which passed to an acute state at the time of the religious Reform, and that not only produced writings and discussions but also wars and massacres, indicates the generality and the strength of our tendency to confuse the divinity with the material and palpable signs that represent her. Fetishism also does have its place in love: the facts assembled in this study will show it.

In this comparison, Binet does not take into account the difference between the fetish, the image, the representation, the symbol, the icon, etc… Rather, he refers to a general tendency to confuse the divinity with the material sign of its representation. Iconoclasm would be the radical means to avoid this confusion and to remove all risk of fetishism.

In its pathological form, contrary to its milder form, fetishism consists in an intense sexual interest that culminates in a genital arousal for inanimate objects, objects which would produce no effect on a normal individual—such as a nightcap, the bindings of ankle-boots, or crisp white aprons. This last example, borrowed from the *Confessions* of Jean-Jacques Rousseau, forms a point of interest in Binet's study, one which he develops at length.

The term "fetishism", Binet claims, is perfectly applicable to this type of sexual perversion. The adoration of inert objects is in many ways reminiscent of the savage's adoration "for fishbones or for bright pebbles. Except for the fundamental difference that in the cult of the sick patient the religious adoration was replaced by a sexual appetite."[2] From that moment onward, Binet is obliged to heavily infuse his discussion with a religious vocabulary in order to speak of this quite peculiar type of "amorous madness" that is fetishism in love. "Cult", "amorous idolatry", "adoration", but also "relic" and "reliquary" are the terms that riddle his analysis.

Thus, when Freud first tackles the question of fetishism, very succinctly, in the 1905 *Three Essays on Sexuality*, the field is far from being new. A subtle analysis has already led Binet to conclusions that bring us closer, not to the

---

[1] Alfred Binet, *Le fétichisme dans l'amour* (Paris : Edition La bibliothèque des Introuvables, 2000).
[2] Ibid.

Freudian interpretation of fetishism from 1927, but to a certain *mode de pensée* which may be considered Freudian. Rather than to heredity, degeneration, or other biological factors, Binet gives priority in the choice of the fetish to what he calls "causalité psychique." Since Binet, the fetishistic *perversion* has been explained by psychological causes: namely, an association of ideas based upon contiguity. And as with the other sexual aberrations, it is the result of a forgotten, fortuitous event, which Binet refers to as an *accident*. However, the accident is not always completely forgotten. Such is the case, for example, with Jean-Jacques Rousseau and Mademoiselle Lambercier's white aprons. While normal love is directed to the totality of the person, the fetishist isolates one part of the person's body (or something in relation to it) in order to make it the primary object of an exclusive erotic cult. A part is substituted for the whole. As a result, we see that fetishism is the adoration of objects that are improper for direct satisfaction of the goals of reproduction.

Thus, it appears that, even before the emergence of psychoanalysis, examining fetishism could introduce an approach that draws very close to the enigma of erotic desire. Fetishism clearly illustrates the uncanniness upon which human desire is founded, and which contradicts all naturalistic or teleological conceptions of sexuality. The absurdity, the incongruity, and the radical singularity of the fetish oblige one to think of human desire not as a physiological function that finds its own law in organic nature, but as being completely subjected to the absurd mechanism of imagination, and thus open to accidental and fortuitous events. Fetishes are the hazards attendant upon the association of ideas (in the empiricist sense that includes images, perceptions, etc...). Thus, as Binet shows very well, the aberrant choice of the fetish and its capacity to nourish the sexual drive and genital satisfaction are to be explained by *psychological causality* and the inference of an *accident*.

That we are forced to resort to the analogy of an exotic sacred in order to name this sexual aberration tells us a great deal regarding the intrinsic exoticism of desire. Human desire is surrealist, so to speak. And it is, without any doubt, this revelation which is so fascinating and so troubling in fetishism. If, in the religious domain, the idol is always the god of others, the sexual fetish reveals in the same way what may be someone else's singular and personal desire in its radical and extravagant oddity.

But then Freud arrives on the scene. Paradoxically, we may assert that he places a limitation on the strangeness of fetishism, insofar as he clarifies its aetiology with a unique explanation. Behind the crazy multiplicity of fetishes lies one psychological law that can explain all of them. The objects are numerous and their choice is fortuitous, but they all have the same function. They are all substitutes for the same thing, or rather, for the same absence of thing, or for the same ghost that haunts them and whose terror they try to exorcise with this pathetic sign of victory.

In the *Three Essays on Sexuality* of 1905, Freud does not go much further than Alfred Binet, whose conclusions he accepts. The psychoanalytic theory of fetishism proper would only be realized much later, in the article ("Fetishism") published in 1927.[3] The theory that Freud cautiously advances is already quite familiar to us. Fetishism always proposes the same general solution. And that solution is: the fetish is a substitute for the penis. Freud is aware of the deceptive character of this explanation. There is, however, a little surprise that could favorably compensate for this deception. The fetish does not refer to any type of penis in general, but to one very particular—because non-existent—penis, namely, the penis of the mother. This is the penis the boy believed in, prior to abandoning his faith. Therefore, this is also a matter of belief; more specifically, of an infantile, deceived belief. The fetish is the substitute for the phallus of the woman (the mother) in which the young child believed—a belief that he does not want to renounce completely.

As we know, the mechanism is as follows: facing the discovery, which occurs in a more or less fortuitous manner, that a woman does not have a penis, the child feels absolute dread, because he is confronted with the possibility of his own castration. That which he fears, he sees realized in a woman, and for the first time he is forced to seriously consider a possibility that had previously troubled him, but which he could nevertheless discount as something unlikely to occur. Facing the horrible revelation that fills him with terror, the child chooses to *negate*, or rather, to *deny*, or even better, to *disavow* what he has seen, despite the risk of contradicting his initial perception. This disavowal (*Verleugnung*), however, cannot completely restore the belief so brutally refuted by the facts. Yes, a woman does possess a penis, but it is not exactly the one in which he initially believed. A substitute object will inherit the interest that was directed to the phallus, the one whose existence seemed so certain, the imagined phallus, that ghost organ to which the child devoted all his belief. And this is how the fetish object is created as a substitute for the phallus that the woman lacks.

I will not develop further the questions raised by Freud concerning this negated, denied, or disavowed perception. These questions concern, for example, whether the refusal to recognize reality, the rejection of perception, and the splitting of the ego that it implies, are identical to the defence mechanisms in psychosis. These questions remain pending in Freud, even in his final work, *An Outline of Psychoanalysis*. For the fetishist, there is no total rejection, but rather a displacement of value, a transfer of the signification of the absent phallus to another object. There is, to a certain extent, a denial or disavowal of sexual difference, but also a compromise between the existence and non-existence of the woman's penis. Moreover, Freud came to realize that the sexual object, even in the non-aberrant case, is always a substitute. The original object of desire is definitively lost. It will be "represented by an endless

[3]   Sigmund Freud, *SE XXI*, 152-7.

series of substitutive objects none of which, however, brings full satisfaction."[4] The particularity of fetishism is that the final object of the sexual drive is a substitute, but this substitute is an inanimate object, detached or detachable.

2. Fetishism and the Trophy in Greek Mythology

We have now arrived at a question that will lead us to a more risky approach. Freud often had recourse to myths, in particular Greek myths, to throw light on his interpretation and sometimes to confirm it. Yet he makes no reference to any myth that could correspond to fetishistic desire. Indeed, it seems that we will not be able to find, in the vast corpus of Greek myths, a direct confirmation of the mechanism of this so-called perversion, nor even a simple illustration of it, even though Greek myths are far from sparing when it comes to the domain of sexual aberrations, whether one considers incest, voyeurism, zoophilia, etc... However, I think there is a possibility to approach fetishism indirectly in Greek mythology, and to find a mechanism that we could consider as regulative. In my interpretation, fetishism would be the aberrant counterpart to, or the exceptional derailment of, this regulative mechanism.

With this in mind, we must admit that Freud does not facilitate our task. He places the story of Oedipus, his most characteristic and explanatory myth, at the heart of psychoanalysis. And yet, the story of King Oedipus, with its tragic end, parricide and incest, is certainly not a regular or normative myth. One may concede that, at a certain, precocious moment of mental life, every masculine subject is haunted, as Freud states, by a parricidal impulse and an incestuous desire. However, it is evident that the story of Oedipus is not the one that can pretend to reveal the standard masculine itinerary, the one that could correspond to the successful solution—mythically successful, I mean— of this libidinal journey. That is perhaps why Lacan comes to say, at the end of his doctrinal course, that the Oedipus myth, and the complex that bears the same name, are of no possible use in psychoanalysis, although in terms of myths, he does not provide an alternative that could enlighten us as to the regular, typical path of the masculine subject. And yet, as I have tried to demonstrate elsewhere (in *Oedipus Philosopher*)[5], there are several Greek myths that present a story that we may say is typical of the male hero. These stories do not end with an incestuous marriage; the hero marries the daughter of a foreign king, a donor-king so to say, who offers at the same time both his kingdom and his daughter.

---

[4] Freud, "On the Universal Tendency to Debasement in the Sphere of Love", *SE XI*, 189.

[5] Jean-Joseph Goux, *Oedipe philosophe* (Paris : Edition Aubier, 1990); English translation, *Oedipus Philosopher*, trans. Catherine Porter (Stanford: Stanford University Press, 1994).

Let us consider briefly the myth of Jason, the myth of Perseus, and that of Bellerophon. These three myths are alike. Utilizing a precise comparison, and placing in parallel the sequences constituting these myths, we may be able to distil a common, minimum narrative core. We may call it the *monomyth*, to borrow a term from James Joyce. Without going into all the details, four main sequences seem to structure these myths. Each hero is threatened by a *first king* at the beginning of his life, or even prior to his life. Later, each one is sent, by a *second king*, to fight a ruthless battle against a female monster. Each hero succeeds in the terrible ordeal with the help of a god or a sage. And finally, each one receives, from a *third king*, as the prize for the successful ordeal, a fiancée whom the hero marries, as well as receiving the kingdom.

Thus, without insisting on the details of the narrative parallel that brings these myths closer together, and without lingering over each sequence and the precise function of the three kings, suffice to say that the scenario always includes a violent murder of a female monster. Victory in this ordeal is the condition for union with the fiancée, which is, in fact, the prize for the victory. After many terrible ordeals, Jason vanquishes the female serpent, keeps the Golden Fleece, and marries Medea; Perseus is the victor of Medusa and of a sea monster, and he weds Andromeda; Bellerophon defeats the chimera and he marries Philonae. It is remarkable that the murder of the female monster and not the murder of the father, as the Freudian theory might have us expect, is at the core of these myths that illustrate the formation of masculine desire. Without any doubt, we could easily broaden the corpus of referential myths beyond the Greek era and still frequently come across the same narrative structure.

It is clear that this monomyth, as we have called it, expresses the typical trajectory of the male subject. This mythical core seems to echo many symbolic or imaginary plans, as a ritual of royal investiture or as a scenario of initiation for young men. Hence there would be a universal, mythico-ritual core, an anthropological invariant in which a consistent pattern could be identified. Moreover, it is striking how closely the myth of Oedipus resembles the monomyth we have just described, insofar as one may articulate a succession of at least formally similar sequences. There are, however, obvious differences as well, since the contents of these sequences are subject to evident distortions.

Obviously, Oedipus does not marry the daughter of a donor-king, but rather he weds his own mother. Furthermore, Oedipus is not challenged to kill a female monster by a mandatory king. At the narrative juncture where the monster would be confronted, Oedipus kills his own father. Moreover, Oedipus does not kill the sphinx in a fierce fight with help from gods and sages; he makes her disappear with the utterance of a single word, a word he finds by his own ingenuity. Thus, the Oedipus myth is an irregular myth, a faulted, disturbed myth in comparison with the typical myth of royal investiture or male initiation. Important consequences for Freudian psychoanalysis may be drawn in reference to the location and the content of these disturbances. But it is not my intention here to comment upon these consequences. Rather, I would like to investigate whether or not fetishism may be clarified, not by the myth of Oedipus, but by the monomyth. This is where the notion of the *trophy* emerges.

In Freud's explanation of fetishism from his 1927 article, "Fetishism", there are many strange expressions used to define the fetish. As the substitute for the phallus that the mother is lacking, the fetish is referred to as a "monument erected by the horror of castration." The fetish is called, even more decisively, the "sign of triumph" over the fear of castration; it is as well a means of protection against that fear. Yet, thus conceived, it is difficult not to view the fetish as closely resembling an extraordinary object, endowed with great powers, which we consistently encounter in all of the standard myths of the hero.

Perseus, after a daring fight with the Gorgons, returns with the head of Medusa, whom he has decapitated. It is a horrible head, seething with a thousand or more serpents, which he brandishes in the face of his enemies in order to petrify them with horror. It is only after this tough, fierce, but victorious battle, and thanks to what is obviously a sign of triumph and a protective object (the head), that he will be able to acquire from the king the beautiful Andromeda, whom he has seen naked and chained to rock, and who has thus enflamed his desire. Similarly, Jason is able to wed Medea only after having gained possession of the Golden Fleece, which he accomplishes through a succession of ordeals that end in a hard-won victory over a female serpent. Finally, Bellerophon is only able to wed Philonae after a dangerous fight against the chimera, a composite, fire-breathing monster. Bellerophon returns with Pegasus, the winged horse, after the ruthless battle. Pegasus is the means of this combat, and the living proof of the hero's victory.

And that is how, in each of these heroic myths, an *object* endowed with great power is earned in the course of a dangerous exploit against a horrifying, female monstrosity. The captured object, which serves as a reminder of the victory, is also the precious pledge that enables him to obtain and marry the fiancée. In the three aforementioned cases, there are important differences in the nature of the object, its powers, and the circumstances that enable it to be obtained. But there is always a common motive: an extraordinary object is captured from the female monstrosity on the occasion of the combat against her. This object is, at one and the same time, a sign of victory, a source of protection, and the pledge required to obtain the desired fiancée. This object is a *talisman* (a word derived from *teles*, belonging to the language of initiation), and it is also—as demonstrated by Louis Gernet concerning the Golden Fleece—an *agalma*, an object endowed with an extreme sacred value. It is also a *trophy*.

Trophy, deriving from the Greek word *tropaion*, is the monument that consecrates the crushing defeat of the enemy, and that is primitively constituted by the mortal remains of that enemy (breast-plate armour, weapons). The word is related to the adjective *trophaios*, which puts to flight, which scares, which casts out devils. Associated with these words, one finds terms linked to the same root: *apotropaios*, protector, saviour; *apotropos*, deflecting horror, avoiding the horrible and terrible. The two characteristics Freud attributes to the fetish—first, the fetish is a monument serving as the sign of triumph over horror; and second, it is protection against a threat—are therefore clearly to be ascertained in the trophy. In the heroic myths of Jason, Perseus, and Bellerophon, one always finds this object, filled with great value, with "the sacred," by which victory may be recognized.

This protective object is the vestige, the memorial to a real combat with the female monster, a difficult, and always fierce, hand-to-hand combat, the outcome of which is victory. The mandatory-king challenges the courageous young male, thinking he will lure him to his death. But the hero overcomes the obstacle, and the trophy with which he returns is the sign of his victorious combat. And yet, it is with this trophy that the hero wins the fiancée who is at stake in the combat, and he obtains her from a foreign donor-king. The hero does not stop at the trophy—it is not the most profound goal of his efforts. Rather, he uses the trophy as a value, *agalma*, the counterpart of which is a woman, a princess, the daughter of a king. The trophy is worth the *entirety* of the future wife, even though it is only a partial remnant of a combat, the metonymy of a fierce, decisive ordeal against the female monster.

Moreover, it is not difficult to see what these myths have to tell us about these female monsters. Born from the watery depths and the earth, an abyssal and dark image, the monster is not the person of the mother, but is located in the dimension of the mother, a horrific and anxiogenic dimension against which the hero must fight in order to free the fiancée. That is to say, he must violently separate the monster-mother from the non-maternal femininity held prisoner by the monster. The absence of a trophy is a significant irregularity of the Oedipus myth, one which contrasts it with the myths of Jason, Perseus, or Bellerophon. Oedipus does not bring anything back, any object, from his victory over the sphinx. This victory is an autodidactic and intellectual victory rather than a bloody and initiatory one.

3. Fetish as Trophy

What can we now affirm regarding the relation between the trophy and the fetish? As Freud claims, the fetish is a sign of triumph and a source of protection. Therefore, the fetish shares some features with the trophy. The fetish also arises from a certain vision of horror, a quick glance at that which one must avoid truly seeing, as when Perseus must find the means not to look at the head of Medusa directly, lest he be petrified. We know that Freud, in regards to Medusa, gives an interpretation of the numerous moving serpents on her head, in the middle of her tousled hair: a fantastic, hallucinatory compensation for the terrifying absence of the penis. This confirms, in this case, the significance of the horror with which Perseus is confronted. It is the same horror as that of the fetishist.

But, in the case of the fetish, contrary to the conquest yielding the trophy, the triumph remains incomplete. The fetish is the sign of a partial triumph, a triumph in *trompe-l'oeil*. The fetish is not the outcome of a separation, of a cut, of a tortured but successfully executed detachment from the monster-mother (which we should call, in Freudian terms, symbolic castration). It is rather the gap, the deviation, the circumvention that allows the pleasure of a partial victory that has been fought to the (symbolic) death. The vertigo of the absence is avoided by the choice of a substitute that diverts the ordeal of symbolic castration, and therefore of the assumption of the (name of the) father according to the law. And while the trophy yields the fiancée as a prize, and thus allows its owner to become king, the fetish is a sign that neither provides a woman in exchange, nor limits pleasure (*jouissance*). For, it is a pleasure without alterity, which focuses on an inert object. Thus, it is a perverted pleasure, in the precise sense that Lacan gives to the notion. In contradistinction to the fetish, the trophy is not the object of sexual desire, but is rather the attestation of complete triumph over the monster-mother (beheading the Medusa). It is the valorous object that opens the way to non-incestuous desire.

If the three references upon which I rely have a common narrative structure, containing the same motives and the same chain of events, they nevertheless accentuate different angles in the conquest of the trophy. That there may exist a strange proximity between the trophy and the fetish can be seen in the myth of Jason, where the Golden Fleece—this precious fur, coveted and guarded by a female serpent, and goal of a long journey—becomes the bridal bed upon which the union of Medea and the hero takes place. In the myth of Perseus, the question of the gaze that kills or petrifies is decisive, as is the blood-covered decapitation. Of course, it is necessary to institute a reversal between the protagonist and that which he encounters: it is not Medusa's gaze that petrifies, but rather that which is seen by the subject. As well, the beheading of Medusa by the hero indicates first a manly combat in which the hero triumphs over the female monster. But this beheading is also his own symbolic castration, the one that enables him painfully to cut his infantile bond with the dark, maternal dimension, thus opening the way to non-incestuous desire.

In the myth of Bellerophon, in the struggle against the chimera, it is less the dangerous vision than the aspect of oral voracity that is accentuated—the breath of flame that bursts from her mouth. Still, this oral ravenousness ascribed to the monster can also be understood as a reversal of primitive oral aggression, which overwhelms the subject from within and which he fears as a deadly retaliation. Hence, this question of aggression makes it possible to distinguish the trophy from the fetish, and to confirm the incompleteness of the fetish in regards to the regulative motif of the trophy.

Freud outlines, in the article of 1927, the ambivalence of the fetishist toward his object. This ambivalence illustrates the division or cleavage of the fetishist's ego in regard to the question of the woman's castration. On the one hand, the fetishist reveres his fetish, and on the other hand, he mistreats it, or he confers negative features upon it which are tantamount to a representation of castration. Hostility and tenderness are combined in various proportions, showing at the same time the denial of castration and its recognition. Freud cites the examples of the cutter of the braid of hair, and of foot fetishism in China, in which may be found the simultaneous mutilation or atrophy of the foot, and its ultimate veneration.

Freud's successors, who have investigated the subject of fetishism in greater depth, all emphasize the dimension of aggression, pre-genital aggression toward the fetish as a denial of, and protection against, the destructive drive aimed at a cherished object.[6] The fetish usually includes an element of violence directed toward the woman: uncomfortable shoes, a tight-squeezing corset, buttons, necklaces, straps that are too tight, etc. This aspect perfectly corroborates the derivative or incomplete status of the fetish with respect to the trophy. The comparison also clarifies the nature of the aggression which is directed toward the fetish.

With the bloody murder of the female monster, the typical hero exhausts his powers of deadly aggression aimed at the dark mother. The trophy, most clearly exemplified by Medusa's head, is the visible proof of a victory accomplished. Anxiety has become violence. The horror of castration has been castrated. It is the active component of a much more complex initiatory situation, most likely including the elements of loss and torture that are not accentuated in the heroic myth. Hence, the heroic ordeal is liberation of the feminine. Once again, the myth of Perseus is the exemplary, mythical illustration: the naked Andromeda is tied to a rock and guarded by a sea-monster. There is a decisive separation between the monstrous and anxiogenic feminine that refers back to the dark mother, and the non-maternal, nuptial feminine that was imprisoned.

[6]   For example, see: William H.Gillespie, "A Contribution to the Study of Fetishism," *International Journal of Psychoanalysis* 21 (1940): 401-15; "The Psycho-analytic Theory of Sexual Deviation with Special Reference to Fetishism", in I. Rosen, ed., *The Pathology and Treatment of Sexual Deviation: A Methodological Approach* (New York: Oxford, 1964), 123-45: Phyllis Greenacre, "Certain Relationships between Fetishism and Faulty Development of the Body Image," *Psychoanalytic Study of the Child* 8 (1953): 79-98; "The Fetish and the Transitional Object," *Psychoanalytic Study of the Child* 24 (1969): 144-164; "Fetishism," in *Sexual Deviations*, ed. Ismond Rosen (London: Oxford University Press, 1979), 79-108: Sylvia Payne, "Some Observations on the Ego Development of the Fetishist," *International Journal of Psychoanalysis* 20 (1939).

In fetishism, the aggression remains incomplete. The fetishist has not yet put an end to the monster-mother. The deadly drive toward the dangerous feminine has not totally succeeded. The fetish is nothing but the sign of an incomplete victory, achieved by a displacement or sidestep, and not by a decisive confrontation, as is the case with the conquest of the trophy. Thus, instead of enjoying the freed woman, the fetishist tries to find satisfaction in the erotic veneration, always tainted with aggression, of a simple object that signifies—in a minor, almost derisory mode—the semi-triumph over horror. Thus, the woman remains a threat to fetishistic desire, even if this threat may be kept at a distance, if not exorcised, by the constitution of the fetish that enables, *in extremis*, *jouissance* geared toward the other sex, yet trapped in a narcissistic fantasy.

On the contrary, the trophy is a sign that the threat of the woman has been overcome, and the episode of victory is relegated to the past—a glorious past in which memory is religiously well-preserved. I would point out the attestation of this preservation in a feature of the cult of the Greeks: the head of the Gorgon Medusa—which is the trophy *par excellence*—is offered by Perseus to the goddess Athena who, in return, places it on her shield. The virgin Athena, daughter of Zeus, city-goddess, goddess of Reason, and even tutelary deity of philosophy, is the image of a feminine dimension shielded from lecherous desire: de-sexualized, de-sensualized, and, so to say, sublimated by the rigorous virginity that is protected by her father and herself. This may be interpreted as follows: in order for the male subject to reach this dimension of Reason, it is necessary that the victorious battle against the horror of Medusa, her decapitation, has taken place. This would confirm, in Greek style, that only symbolic castration enables access to the Law, which here may be identified with Reason. But an even more radical solution, one that takes us back to the beginning of this exposé, and that I will stress in a single phrase, is the following: to empty the temple of all images. All that could remind one of the veneration of a sensible object, whatever it may be, is thereby removed, and in this way desire is subjected to a Law of Alterity, a domain of transcendence, in which the subject has no hold, no means to exercise his whim.

If the phenomenon of fetishism—rare in its acute form, but common it its diffuse forms—arouses our vivid interest, it is because it represents so-called perversion in its purest form. If we define it, as Lacan does, as a relation that dissolves the otherness of the other by turning it into an object, or into an "idol", as he says (without, however, the desiring subject ever being satisfied with this dissolution), then the fetish represents the extreme limit of this objectification. But without the comparison between the fetish and the trophy, it is difficult to understand the notion of a sacred object, *agalma*, which is very different from the sexually deviant fetish.

GENITAL CONSTRUCTIONS:
A CRITIQUE OF FREUD'S "FETISHISM"

Andreas De Block

A great deal of the popular literature claims that Freud wrestled with a single question his entire life: "What does a woman want"? This is not an inaccurate representation of affairs. Freud himself wrote that the woman and her sexuality form a dark continent upon which psychoanalysis has never, or at least rarely, set foot. At the same time, however, one must not be misled into thinking that the instinctual life of men was without its secrets for Freud. In many of his later works he extensively, though at the same time hesitantly, examined questions specifically concerned with male sexuality, such as the homosexual ("feminine") position toward the father, the positive Oedipus complex and castration anxiety. From a certain perspective one may even posit that Freud continually sought an answer to the question, "What does a man want"? More specifically, it seems that he was unable to understand why men, in spite of everything, still sometimes desire women.

People who distrust psychoanalysis, but who have no similar misgivings regarding women, generally believe that the first problem, "What does a woman want," may be resolved quite easily: women often just want shoes.[1] Curiously enough, the psychoanalytic answer to the second question, "Why do men still desire women," is strikingly similar: because of their shoes. Stated otherwise, all male genital sexuality seems to be supported by a fetish. I will first explain how Freud came to this conclusion and which philosophical consequences and considerations are associated with it. More specifically, I will first sketch the place Freud allotted to fetishism in his oft-revised *Three Essays on Sexuality* (1905). Thereafter, I will address Freud's actual theory of fetishism as developed in the short articles, "Fetishism" (1927) and "The Splitting of the Ego in the Process of Defense" (1938). I will then direct my attention to the problematic aspects of his theory of fetishism. More specifically, I will argue that the mechanism of disavowal (*Verleugnung*)— introduced by Freud in order to understand the peculiar attitude of the fetishist—is actually redundant. In the final section I will examine the hidden motives behind the fetishistic object choice. Freud believed that castration anxiety played a decisive role in the displacement of the libido to incidental objects. The alternative that I will defend, on the contrary, will push boredom to the fore as the determining affect for fetishistic sexuality.

---

[1] Cf. the Dutch title of the popular-science bestseller by Allan and Barbara Pease: *Why Men Lie and Women always Buy Shoes* (*Waarom mannen liegen en vrouwen altijd schoenen kopen*). English title: *Why Men Lie and Women Cry.*

1. No Fetishistic Instinct

In his *Three Essays on Sexuality* Freud attacks the "popular view of sexuality." This popular view defines sexuality as an instinct: (a) that first arises in puberty; (b) that is directed to an adult person of the opposite sex, and; (c) that has genital union and satisfaction as its goal. As is well known, Freud contests this popular view with the following notions: (a) children have their own sexuality; (b) various objects can exert sexual attraction, and; (c) there are a wide variety of sexual aims. In the first essay Freud concentrates on the last two elements of his sexual theory. More specifically, he argues that the different sexual aberrations, also called perversions or paraphilias, demonstrate that human sexuality should not be considered an exclusively heterosexual and genital instinct. Homosexuality shows that, for some people, individuals of the same sex may be equally or even more seductive than individuals of the opposite sex, while the existence of voyeurism and sadism makes clear that looking and injuring can be sexual aims.

Naturally, Freud's position is only philosophically relevant provided these "aberrations" are more than mere aberrations. The perversions Freud discusses in the *Three Essays* must be more than merely intriguing or sensational examples of what can go wrong with human sexuality. They must be constitutive of human sexuality *as such*. According to Freud, this is precisely the case:

> No healthy person, it appears, can fail to make some addition that might be called perverse to the normal sexual aim; and the universality of this finding is in itself enough to show how inappropriate it is to use the word perversion as a term of reproach. In the sphere of sexual life we are brought up against peculiar and, indeed, insoluble difficulties as soon as we try to draw a sharp line to distinguish mere variations within the range of what is physiologically from pathological symptoms.[2]

With respect to the foundation of the libido, this means that the sexual instinct is an amalgamation of different partial and perverse impulses. The *libido sexualis* consists of oral, anal, genital, voyeuristic, sadistic, homosexual and coprophilic tendencies, which means that they are innate, universally human and already active in childhood.

Freud hereby shows that the distinction between perverse and normal individuals is in part quantitative, and is in part a matter of "manifest versus repressed." Nevertheless, in Freud's theory there is no absolute one-to-one relation between perversions and sexual instincts. Paedophilia, bestiality and fetishism are indeed sexual aberrations—more or less comprehensively detailed in the *Three Essays*—but in the entirety of Freud's *oeuvre* there is no

---

[2]   Sigmund Freud, *SE VII*, 160-1.

trace to be found of paedophilic, zoophilic or fetishistic instincts. How is this to be explained?

In the first place, it is striking that these three aberrations, as in homosexuality, have a connection to an object. But contrary to homosexuality, paedophilia and bestiality are not generally human: not every individual has either manifest or repressed sexual feelings for children and animals. This is sufficient for Freud, in accordance with his biological premises, not to postulate any separate instinct for these perversions. Hence, they seem to owe their inclusion in the *Three Essays* solely to the fact that they give Freud the opportunity to emphasize once again the variability of the sexual object. This explanation is at least partially insufficient with regard to fetishism. On the one hand, fetishism also demonstrates that human sexuality is not bound to one type of object, and that sexual objects can even be found outside the natural sphere. On the other hand, fetishism is indeed universal, at least among the male population.[3] Freud proposes explicitly that even the so-called "normal" individual is in need of a fetish: "A certain degree of fetishism is ... habitually present in normal love, especially in those stages of it in which the normal sexual aims seems unattainable or its fulfilment prevented."[4] Why, then, does he refuse to introduce a fetishistic instinct?

Two elements most likely play a decisive role in this regard. First is the high degree of variability of fetishistic objects, extending from shoes, to lingerie, to locks of hair. This variability seems to suggest that a "unifying" theory of fetishism should be based upon associative and defense mechanisms rather than on one single (infantile) impulse. In this sense, sexual fetishes are, in the first place, seen by Freud as symbols and symptomatic constructions. Secondly, and in association with the first, the fetish is often only a springboard to another object. This is particularly applicable to the less pathological expressions of fetishism. In such cases the fetish is little more than a surrogate for what is truly desired on the basis of genital, masochistic, voyeuristic, or other impulses. People presume that they are, for example, provisionally satisfied with a necklace from the beloved, in anticipation of actual genital pleasure. This means that fetishism is, at most, a displaced sexual interest, for which no separate instinct needs to be postulated. Now, a

---

[3] Freud never unequivocally answers the question whether female fetishism is possible. He does come to the judgment, in 1909, that all women are clothes fetishists (Freud 1988), while his explanation of fetishism from 1927 turns it into an exclusively male affair. Nonetheless, one could argue that the version from 1927 makes it possible to connect male fetishism with the female passion for fashion. The female passion for clothing may, after all, simply be seen as a method to conform to male fetishism. For an extensive discussion of this theme, see: J. Matlock, "Masquerading Women, Pathologized Men: Cross-Dressing, Fetishism, and the Theory of Perversion, 1882-1935," in *Fetishism as Cultural Discourse*, ed. E. Apter and W. Pietz, (Ithica: Cornell University Press, 1993), 31-61.

[4] Freud, *SE VII*, 154.

number of extremely important theoretical questions flow from the view of fetishism as a displaced phenomenon: (1) what motivates displacement? (2) which impulses are displaced? and (3) how does this displacement, at least for the time being, come to a standstill and lead to fixation on a fetish?

(1) In the *Three Essays on Sexuality*, Freud argues that displacement is primarily a result of sexual overvaluation. He describes this process as follows:

> It is only in the rarest instances that the psychical valuation that is set on the sexual object, as being the goal of the sexual instinct as desired target, stops short at its genitals. The appreciation extends to the whole body of the sexual object and tends to involve every sensation derived from it... . This sexual overvaluation is something that cannot be easily reconciled with a restriction of the sexual aim to union of the actual genitals ...[5]

The libido indeed has privileged objects, but it is not very discriminating: should its power be too great to be bound by "actual" objects—or if the object for one reason or another cannot be possessed—then it spreads out and contaminates objects or ideas associated with the actual object. It makes no difference whether these new objects are bodily (foot), psychical (humor), natural (hair), or artificial (clothing). At the origin of fetishism is a deification or overvaluation of the entire individual: fetishism is based on the fact that sexuality is, by definition, polytheistic.[6]

(2) This overvaluation primarily concerns the genital instincts. Only in the event that the genitals are either inadequate, or simply unattainable, do other objects become eligible for libidinous investments. This seems to make fetishism *de facto* a matter of adult sexuality, since the genital instincts, at least according to Freud, only become sexually active from the time of puberty. This, of course, does not hinder the possibility that other, more infantile impulses come to be dragged along in the fetishistic displacement. After all, pubertal and post-pubertal genital sexuality receive contributions from other sources of desire, especially if these can be reconciled with the genital primacy.

(3) The third question concerns what fixates the fetish. Freud approaches this question with caution, presumably because the degree of fixation on the fetish differs from individual to individual. In the *Three Essays*, Freud distinguishes three types of fixation. In the first case there is, in fact, hardly any reference to fixation. Whatever has some relation to the desired object

---

[5] Ibid., 150-1.

[6] Freud's theory actually builds on the schema Binet proposed in his article, "*Le fétichisme dans l'amour.*" According to Binet, fetishism was a monotheism that must be qualified as a perversion because it indicates a betrayal of the polytheism of true love (Binet 1887, 164-5). Freud only adds to this that polytheism is, at the same time, the necessary precondition for fetishistic monotheism.

comes to be accepted as a libidinal substitute precisely because it is in relation to the desired object. A fetishist with this type of fixation reasons as follows: if she has but touched/worn/seen it, it becomes valuable and erotically attractive. The second type is considerably less flexible regarding its choice of fetish. In this case, only women with a certain characteristic (an *"einziger Zug"* or distinguishing mark) are found to be sexually attractive. One is still sexually interested in the entire object, but this interest is provoked and made possible by the presence of a fetishistic feature, for instance, long hair, high heels, or a funereal tone of voice. The third type reveals an even more exclusive object-choice: the fetish alone is important; everything else is redundant. As in the second type, sexual attention is stimulated by a partial object, but unlike in the second type, that partial object no longer refers to other partial objects or to the total object. The fixation is, so to speak, absolute. It is only in this case that Freud actually speaks of pathology.

There is nevertheless, in the second type, also a fixation on the level of the fetish: one is, to be sure, still interested in something other than the fetish, but at the same time, there is only one partial object that can arouse interest for that other thing. Freud attributes the immense erotic effect of that particular object to a combination of early childhood experiences and the activities of what he calls "symbolic thought processes." This means that the fixation on the fetish resembles closely the formation of a neurotic compromise or symptom. Why is this? The fetishistic fixation is preceded by a more original object that has been abandoned, despite the displeasure that results from this loss. Thereafter, a different object is invested with the same power, or with a power derived from the original. The object has this power because it in one way or another resembles the original object, yet it produces less displeasure.

In his concrete reconstruction of the fetish choice or fixation, Freud, as usual, proceeds with little subtlety: the original object was the female genital and the fetish symbolizes that female genital: "The foot is an ancient sexual symbol, often found in mythology, fur thanks its role as fetish undoubtedly due to the association with the hair of the *mons Veneris*." In the *Three Essays on Sexuality*, Freud does not offer a convincing explanation as to why the female genital carries such disturbing effects along with it. This question will become central to the conclusions drawn in his 1927 article, "Fetishism", and will incite him to amend his initial theory of fetishism.

2. The phallic fetish

The reprinted editions of the *Three Essays on Sexuality* from 1910, 1915, and 1920 contain numerous additions to the original. Freud adds several footnotes concerning the determination or overdetermination of the fetish, where he points out that coprophilic pleasure in smells, and the repression of this pleasure, are important in the choice of the fetish.[7] Freud now believes that he can explain why dirty and vile-smelling feet are the primary objects of sexual interest, as is the case in foot fetishism. However, he immediately nuances this explanation [*Added 1910*]:

> Another factor that helps toward explaining the fetishistic preference for the foot is to be found among the sexual theories of children: the foot represents a woman's penis, the absence of which is deeply felt. [*Added 1915:*] In a number of cases of foot-fetishism it has been possible to show that the scopophilic instinct, seeking to reach its object (originally the genitals) from underneath, was brought to a halt in its pathway by prohibition and repression. For that reason it became attached to a fetish in the form of a foot or shoe, the female genitals (in accordance with the expectations of childhood) being imagined as male ones.[8]

Freud elaborates this view in his essay on fetishism from 1927.

In "Fetishism," Freud suggests that infantile sexual "theories" form the basis of fetishism in general and the fetishistic object choice in particular. More specifically, he holds infantile fantasies about the phallic woman, and about castration as punishment, responsible for the fact that many heterosexual men are steered in the direction of fetishism. This suggests that the young boy's original heterosexual interest is confronted with the fact that the female genital differs from what was expected. The female has no phallus. This does

[7]   Its importance is illustrated in Freud's analysis of a number of fetishistic case studies presented during the meeting of the Vienna Psychoanalytic Society on February 24, 1909. In a case of boot fetishism, Freud explains as follows: "the patient had been in the habit of digging between his toes, where they emit a strong-smelling secretion, which evidently must be an object of pleasure for man, i.e. the pleasure from smells, which lasts until disgust enters in and puts an end to it. A portion of anal eroticism consists also in this, i.e., in the custom on the part of the individual of working his finger into his anus and then smelling it... . This pleasure from smells belongs among those impulses which are for the most part repressed. Persons who once got enjoyment from foul-smelling foot secretions, and in whom this partial repression of impulse occurred, become foot fetishists, in that the pleasure from odors is suppressed, while the odorless foot is idealized. In the ideal, odor is no longer an issue, it is not even emphasized negatively... . Here we find again a lost instinctual pleasure, but here the *direct object* of its complex is separated from the instinct and rises to a fetish." This explanation reveals two notable differences from the footnote in the *Three Essays*. First, the foot here is not a substitute for a more original libidinous object. The original object *is* the fetish. The only change the sexual preference has undergone consists in the fact that the olfactory interest no longer plays a central role. One initially chose the foot despite the (evil) smell, but in adult fetishism, sexual interest is fixated on the foot, irregardless whether it stinks or not. This is as well the second difference from the passage in the *Three Essays on Sexuality*. There Freud proposes that in fetishism, only foul-smelling objects (feet, footwear, locks of hair, undergarments) are sexually attractive.

[8]   Freud, *SE VII*, 155.

not directly lead him to give up the fantasy of the phallic woman. On the contrary, the child retains this fantasy and interprets the absence as the result of a forceful intervention: the woman has been castrated. Where the phallus once was, there is a wound, and that wound was inflicted as punishment for something the woman did wrong. This interpretation is above all painful because it means that his own, male genital is no longer safe. Such an interpretation makes the father's threat of castration all the more real. The discovery that the woman has no phallus is, on the one hand, constitutive for male (sexual) identity. On the other hand, however, it awakens the idea that sexual identity has an arbitrary character: one can lose it. Fetishism solves this problem by denying the painful impression. More specifically, the fetishist disavows the perceived castration of the female by constructing a new female phallus, the fetish.

Freud's explanation in "Fetishism" differs on a number of important points from the theory that he put forward in the *Three Essays*. First of all, the fetish is no longer a symbol for the vagina, but for the female phallus. The phallic fetish does not receive its symbolic value on the basis of visual or olfactory resemblance, but principally from a regressive temporal movement: "It seems rather that when the fetish is instituted some process occurs which reminds one of the stopping of a memory in traumatic amnesia. As in this latter case, the subject's interest comes to a halt half-way, as it were; it is as though the last impression before the uncanny and traumatic one is retained as the fetish."[9] Secondly, it follows from the explanation in "Fetishism" that the displacement constitutive for fetishism is a dynamic rather than an economic question. Sexual interest does not spontaneously develop of its own accord. On the contrary, it is displaced from its original object provided the existence of strong affective motives. Fetishism is a result of a defense mechanism and not the outcome of natural association.

The question that most occupies Freud in "Fetishism" concerns the very nature of this defense. Is disavowal a sort of repression, or is it a matter of very different defense mechanisms? At first glance, the fetishistic defense seems closely related to the narcissistic processes typical for the psychoses. In fetishism, as in the psychoses, the Ego's wishes are taken as reality. The fetishist's wish triumphs over reality precisely there where, for the neurotic, the reality principle comes to the fore. Nevertheless, Freud does not draw the conclusion that fetishism would therefore be a psychotic disorder. This primarily has to do with the very ambiguous approach of the fetishist toward what is, for him, a painful reality. According to Freud, there exists in the fetishist's psyche yet another attitude alongside the attitude that squares with the wish, namely, the attitude that actually takes account of reality.[10] On the

---

9   Freud, *SE XXI*, 155.
10   In fact, it is more than just a matter of two desired realities existing side-by-side. On the basis of the wish, reality is actually *denied*, while, on the other hand,

one hand, the fetishist disavows female castration. But on the other hand, and simultaneously, he also acknowledges it. Freud calls this process "splitting."[11]

In the opening line of the short and unfinished article, "Splitting of the Ego in the Process of Defense" (1940), Freud suggests that his solution for the psychodynamic problem of fetishism is ingenious, innovative, and clarifying. Nevertheless, the mechanism of "splitting" in many ways remains uncertain and even debatable. Freud leaves unresolved[12] whether or not this defense: (a) only applies to fetishism; (b) plays a role in all perversions, or; (c) also appears outside the domain of perversion. A second, more fundamental objection claims that the simultaneous existence of knowing and not-knowing is not exclusive to fetishism. One also finds it in neuroses and other pathologies. This becomes clear when one considers the fact that the fetishist—certainly on the conscious level—holds no contradictory *theories* regarding whether or not the woman has been castrated. The knowing and not-knowing in question are in no way intellectual.

But what does Freud mean then when he proposes that the fetishist, on the one hand, avows that the woman is castrated, and on the other hand still retains the contradictory infantile fantasy by means of the fetish? Perhaps he intends to do nothing more than provide some consistency to the ambiguous or irrational *attitude* of the fetishist. This attitude implies that men hold the woman in contempt, yet still desire her through a detour. The fetish forms a compromise between these two attitudes: men humiliate the woman by divinizing a part of her. If Freud believes he needs to postulate a mechanism other than repression in order to account for the fact that the symptom is a more or less classic compromise formation, then in my opinion that has everything to do with the enjoyment of the symptom (the fetish). After all, whereas the neurotic symptom in general causes more suffering than pleasure, on the whole the fetish is not experienced as problematic by the fetishist. Freud begins his article "Fetishism" with the remark that the fetishists whom he had treated in analysis do not complain of dissatisfaction with their "sexual abnormality": "Usually they are quite satisfied with it, or even praise the way

---

reality also *asserts itself* in the wish. This attitude is not typified by a sort of psychical indecisiveness. On the contrary, there are two reactions to one problem: "[The ego] must now decide either to recognize the real danger, give way to it and renounce the instinctual satisfaction, or disavow reality and make itself believe that there is no reason to fear, so that it may be able to retain the satisfaction ... the child takes neither course, *or rather* he takes both simultaneously, which comes to the same thing." Freud, "Splitting of the Ego in the Process of Defense," *SE XXI*, 275, emphasis added.

[11] Freud, "Fetishism," *SE XXI*, 156.
[12] In the *Outline of Psychoanalysis* (1940), Freud describes splitting as an automatic result of nearly every defense mechanism. In "Fetishism" and "Splitting of the Ego in the Process of Defense" he applies splitting to cases that seem to be more neurotic than perverse (fetishistic) or psychotic.

in which it eases their erotic life."[13] Like other neurotic or psychotic symptoms, the fetish comes into existence as a reaction to a specific problem, but contrary to the other symptoms, the fetish is a happy symptom: this symptom, in effect, produces less suffering than the problem to which it was the answer. This appears mainly from the fact that the fetish is the necessary and sufficient condition for (manifest) sexual pleasure, while the other symptoms are barriers or, at best, paltry substitutes for such pleasure. This implies that two conflicting tendencies in the ego can both be satisfied without a loss of pleasure or reality: *one disavows the worth of the woman by avowing the value of her shoes*. Consequently, what Freud calls "splitting" seems above all to be a synthesis.

In the following section I will examine: (1) what affects are synthesized by this splitting and; (2) if this splitting is actually constitutive for every case of sexual fetishism. These two questions deal directly with the driving motives behind the fetishistic interest.

3. Humiliation, anxiety, or boredom?

Prima facie, there are two conflicting interpretations concerning the affective motives of fetishistic splitting. One could argue—and this is the first interpretation—that the flesh is threatening *per se*. Meaning tends to disappear when one is in too direct, suffocating contact with one's own embodiment and the embodiment of the other. In this interpretation, fetishism may be considered as protection against the meaninglessness or anonymity of pure physicality. The fetish creates the distance necessary for developing meaning-giving mechanisms, which then acquire free rein. Pure nature then finds itself on the losing side, even in the domain that seems pre-eminently hers: sexuality. The fetish provides animal sexuality with a human face. Or again: the fetish subjectifies the objectifying activity that always penetrates the genital relation. But is this actually the core around which fetishism turns? Can one effortlessly translate what Freud refers to as castration anxiety into an anxiety for the disappearance of identity into undifferentiated embodiment?

There is, however, a second interpretation of fetishistic splitting, and my interpretation has, I think, more in common with this one than with the first. At least *at first sight*, the motives behind the splitting that I have emphasized have nothing to do with anxiety and everything to do with an aversion to, or a liking for, the woman. Actually, they are in perfect agreement with feminist discourse, insofar as the fetishist degrades the woman by reducing her to what she wears or what she has, and in no way takes into account what she is. Thanks to the fetish, the man may satisfy his heterosexual instincts without having to recognize the woman as an aim or as a person. He exerts power over

---

13   Freud, "Fetishism," *op. cit.*, 152.

the woman by means of the fetish. This is made evident, for instance, by female subjection to the (male) fashion industry, which convinces her that she derives her value from what she wears. Consequently, from a feminist perspective the fetishistic attitude is clearly objectifying, and not in the least affirmative of the woman's subjectivity. Fetishism makes the woman even more anonymous than she was on the basis of male, phallocentric impulses.

It is possible to reconcile the idea that fetishism inserts a meaning into sexuality with the feministic view of fetishism, according to which the fetishist objectifies the woman. The synthesis suggests that the objectification of the woman flows unavoidably from the affirmation of male subjectivity and identity. The woman is, however, no *accidental* victim, since her corporality confronts the man with the meaninglessness and contingency of that to which he attributes all value: the phallus. On the one hand, this turns the fetish into a means to avenge himself on the woman for the anxiety and uncertainty that she unleashed in the male mind. On the other hand, the denigration of the woman by means of the fetish is also the ideal manner to annihilate one's own anxiety and uncertainty: as long as the fetishist can dominate the woman, his identity is secured. Anxiety, domination, and identity form a nearly inextricable knot.

The view that synthesizes both interpretations approximates closely the Freudian theory of fetishism. The only thing it neglects is the specificity of fetishism. One may, after all, propose that almost every perverse individual uses, out of anxiety, a sexually tinted violence in order to ensure his identity. In this sense, there is actually little difference between the sadist, the voyeur, and the fetishist. Freud solves this problem by considering the most important perversions from the perspective of the attitude taken against castration. The sadist and the masochist attempt to avert and control anxiety by repeating the activity of castration. The voyeur and the exhibitionist, on the other hand, emphasize that they are indifferent to castration: they seek or show precisely what was or may be the object of castration. The fetishist considers castration as something that never happened and never will happen, insofar as even the woman possesses a phallus, albeit not in the place where it was initially expected.

In short, Freud is able to synthesize and go beyond the prevailing theories of fetishism because he considers the structural function of castration and castration-anxiety. Nevertheless, this synthetic view still remains somewhat unsatisfactory. This has not so much to do with the overly concrete character of Freud's speculations about the castration complex, but rather with the fact that Freud, in 1927, described fetishism as a "perversion" in the classic psychiatric sense; strictly divorced from other perversions and from so-called "normal" adult sexuality. In this text, fetishism is indeed defined as a specific answer to a general human problem (castration, sexual difference) for which, *de facto*, numerous answers are possible. Freud states it as follows: "Probably no male human being is spared the fright of castration at the sight of a female genital. Why some people become homosexual as a consequence of that impression, while others fend it off by creating a fetish, and the great majority surmount it, we are frankly not able to explain."[14] Thus, according to the text from 1927, fetishism is indeed a human possibility, but this does not mean that it is a possibility that is always realized: one can also deal with the fundamental problem by becoming a homosexual, a voyeur, or just by becoming normal. A view such as this is problematic above all because, in fact, no form of sexuality is devoid of fetishistic elements, as Freud had remarked in the *Three Essays*. Not only perverse fetishists are excited by high heels and black lingerie, and it is difficult to call the fascination homosexuals have for leather and little sailor suits as anything other than fetishistic.

Prima facie, these objections may easily be refuted by pointing out that Freud, in "Fetishism," envisioned only the 'structural' perversion, and that this does not necessarily mean that neurotic sexuality can be devoid of perverse elements. One could, for example, point to the fact that alongside perverse voyeurism there might also be a voyeurism that more or less, and without difficulty, submits to genital primacy. In other words, the other perversions also have structural and 'transstructural' variants. Yet there is still an important difference between voyeurism and sadism on the one hand, and fetishism on the other, for which this solution to the proposed problem does not suffice. Contrary to fetishism, voyeurism and sadism have their roots in a (partial) drive, from which it follows that they are indeed unavoidable for every sexualized subject. Everyone must do something with their sadism and voyeurism. Some, to the extent possible, unify these impulses with their other sexual tendencies; others give them a new value and meaning by using them as an answer to *per se* unanswerable questions; and still others banish them to the unconscious. Fetishism is not transstructural in the same way. This may be ascertained, for example, from the fact that, as Lacan correctly pointed out, there is no neurotic fetishism. Fetishism in the case of neurotics always takes part in their manifest sexuality and can never be constitutive for their neuroses, precisely because fetishism cannot be repressed. But how then is one to explain the peculiar transstructural character of fetishism? Which factors ensure that both the pervert and the neurotic are heavily dependent for their sexual pleasure on something that, from a naturalistic perspective, can only be seen as a surrogate?

There are different answers to these questions. First, one may argue that the unity among the different forms of fetishism is merely superficial. This means that the different varieties of fetishism ultimately have fundamentally different conditions and motives. Ordinary fetishism is therefore seen as the result of quasi-natural sexual associations, which Freud addressed in the *Three Essays*, while perverse fetishism usually or even exclusively must be understood as a narcissistic defense against the threatening confrontation with sexual difference. The perverse fetishist wishes to completely disregard the

---

[14]   Ibid., 154.

female genital. The everyday fetishist, on the other hand, does not want to allow the female genital to limit his interests. Second, one may argue that the sexual craving for stimulation found in ordinary fetishism forms the springboard to the perverse variety. *In concreto*, this implies that no one is satisfied with the genital alone, but that some, after a period of time, and after the intervention of painful experiences, can simply no longer return to the original object.

Against these two answers it may be objected that they testify to an inadequate understanding of normal fetishism. The craving for stimulation of the average fetishist is, in fact, never a desire for something more than the genital; rather, it is always a desire for something other than the genital. Stated otherwise: the genital turns everyone off. Hardly anyone is sexually interested in a man or a woman owing to that individual's sexual organs. From this perspective—and possibly only from this perspective—the sexologists are correct when they assert that "size does not matter." In non-perverse sexuality as well, the focus on the genital is primarily a displacement of the focus on the fetish, and not the other way around!

At first sight this objection has no seriously damaging consequences for the theory laid out in "Fetishism"—quite to the contrary. On the grounds of this conclusion, one may indeed move to the generalized theory of fetishism, which differs from Freud's view only insofar as it emphasizes that *nobody* overcomes the horror of castration. *Everyone* will split and every fetish will be an ambiguous memorial to the belief in the phallic woman. In other words, a similar, generalized theory of fetishism results in the reduction of transstructural fetishism to structural fetishism. Naturally, one could reply that even if some forms of fetishism are strongly differentiated from others, these differences are either gradual or are the effect of an interaction between fetishism and other pathological tendencies in the individual.

From a Freudian perspective, there is, in fact, little to object to this view. It fits together seamlessly with the anthropo-psychiatric undertone of much of Freud's work, which raises "pathological" fetishism to a constitutive element of all (male) sexuality. This intratheoretical coherence does not necessarily mean, however, that the generalized theory of fetishism is philosophically convincing. First of all, it appears that the existence of homosexual fetishism puts this theory under significant pressure. Why, in fact, would a homosexual need a fetish if he has found another means perfectly suitable for eliminating the memory of castration anxiety? Secondly, it appears that the "normal" fetishist does not have to overcome an aversion or fear of the female genital. Rather, he has to overcome *boredom*. The female wound does not repel him; it simply interests him in a very moderate and short-lived manner. Of course, one could view this disinterest in the genital as prolonging the defensive stance of original disgust for it, but such an *ad hoc* explanation can only be valid, in my opinion, if there is no plausible alternative. And one may doubt whether such a plausible alternative actually exists.

Perhaps if we want to have a better understanding of normal hetero- and homosexual fetishism we should turn our attention to interpersonal relations that are not so narrowly sexual. These relations are also often based upon interest for inessential factors. People establish friendships with others because they wear the 'right' shoes or the 'right' pants, or play the 'right' sport. These factors or activities are 'right' because they reveal something about how a person is or might be as a friend: they are expressions of character, education and temperament. It does not seem far-fetched to suppose that something similar occurs in the formation of sexual relationships and contacts. In essence, this means little more than that men are sexually interested in women wearing high heels because they suppose, or hope, that this is a sign of their fiery character, and not so much because men may momentarily forget or disavow castration because of this particular footwear. The same may be said—*mutatis mutandis*—for other fetishes such as blond hair, lace lingerie, leather, and so on. From this perspective, sexual disinterest in the genitals is even easier to explain, considering that one can deduce little from the sight of the genitals regarding matters that are truly important in sex: age, qualities as a lover or mother (father), sense of adventure, submissiveness ...

As in Freud's theory of fetishism from the *Three Essays*, this interpretation also emphasizes the importance of associations for the existence of fetishistic interests. Otherwise than Freud, however, I propose that the different fetishes—at least in so-called normal fetishism—do not symbolize the genitals, but are rather "indices" or "markers" of diverse, non-genital (though not necessarily asexual) qualities. This does not definitively exclude that the fixation on fetishes and the qualities they refer to may be the result of a complex interaction of early childhood impressions, traumatic experiences, defense mechanisms and biology, such as Freud often defended. But it does mean that the castration complex is less decisive for normal sexuality than is often thought in psychoanalytic circles. Or again: fetishes are certainly not always genital constructions.

4. Conclusion

In the *Three Essays on Sexuality*, Freud uses fetishism principally to illustrate a number of points from his sexual theory, such as the objectless character of the libido and the importance of sexual overvaluation in the formation of perversions. These points are rendered concrete through a highly descriptive and less psychodynamic approach to the relevant phenomena. On the contrary, in the texts from 1927 and 1938, the psychodynamics of perverse fetishism occupy the central position. More specifically, in these short articles Freud demonstrates that the mechanism of splitting is fundamental for the genesis of the fetishistic attitude and the fixation on a fetishistic object. By means of this splitting, the fetishist assumes a position with respect to the castration complex, a position that differs fundamentally from the neurotic and psychotic positions.

In this essay, I have intended to demonstrate that the perverse fetishistic position does not significantly differ from the neurotic position. Disavowal and splitting are—as I read them—in fact little more than retranslations of older notions that seem adequate for the explanation of neurotic pathogenesis, namely, repression and compromise formation. Furthermore, something strange occurs in fetishism that might incline one to give this perversion a special place in psychoanalytic nosology. Freud's description of the ambiguous attitude of the fetishist suggests, namely, that the compromise formation in fetishism takes part in manifest sexuality, something that is emphatically ruled out with neurotic pathologies. If, in fetishism, the symptom exists under the primacy of the genitals, then the neurotic generally has great difficulty reconciling his symptoms with his manifest sexual life. The real question, in fact, is whether this view is easy to generalize. It is often more fruitful, I believe, to simply explain fetishistic interests on the basis that the fetish contains considerable informative value about the quality of a potential sexual partner, rather than on the basis of psychodynamic revisions. The fetish is, in other words, still a symbol, but not always a symptom.

WHAT'S SO FUNNY ABOUT FETISHISM?

Mignon Nixon

> The euphoria which we endeavor to reach by these means is nothing other than the mood of a period of life in which we were accustomed to deal with our psychical work with a small expenditure of energy—the mood of our childhood, when we were ignorant of the comic, when we were incapable of jokes, and when we had no need of humor to make us feel happy in our life.
> Freud, *Jokes and Their Relation to the Unconscious*

Fetishism is funny. The sexual fetishist has odd tastes, sexual fetishes are risible, and the practice of fetishism is the butt of jokes. In its more esoteric, or aesthetic, forms, fetishism can elicit a mocking humor by being itself so devoid of fun. In its denial of reality and stubborn devotion to the lost object, which is also the very object of anxiety, aesthetic fetishism lends itself to parody and pastiche. If, then, fetishism is a source of cultural amusement, is it possible to explain what's so funny about fetishism in psychoanalytic terms?

Freud hints at this possibility by means of an association. For side-by-side with his essay on fetishism, and written in the same month of August 1927, is the one on humor. Humor, Freud observes, is a strategy that asserts the pleasure principle against reality such that trauma is displaced by pleasure, yields to the ego's insistence that "traumas are no more than occasions for it [the ego] to gain pleasure."[1] It is the superego, Freud contends, that rises to the occasion, adopting a parental attitude toward the child-like ego and triumphantly turning trauma into an excuse for pleasure. He offers the example of gallows humor, the ultimate test of humor as a mechanism of defense. The subject achieves a sort of mastery over the trauma, a nonpathological denial whose effects Freud describes as rebellious, liberating, and elevating.[2]

Somewhat like the humorist, the fetishist is split. He employs the fetish object both to refuse reality and to redeem it. Enacting the psychic division in which the fetishist simultaneously recognizes and disavows castration, the fetish therefore is an ambivalent object: it encapsulates, in Octave Mannoni's celebrated formulation, the contradiction "Je sais bien, mais quand même": I

---

[1] Sigmund Freud, "Humor," in *SE XXI*, 162.
[2] For a brief but suggestive discussion of the parental role of the superego in humor as a specifically maternal agency, operating counter to the usually repressive and prohibitive function of the paternal superego, see Susan Rubin Suleiman, "Playing and Motherhood; or, How to Get the Most out of the Avant-Garde," in *Representations of Motherhood*, ed. Donna Bassin, Margaret Honey, and Meryle Mahrer Kaplan (New Haven: Yale University Press, 1994), 279.

know very well (that the woman lacks a penis), but nevertheless (I prefer to think of her as having one). For in the scenario Freud describes, fetishism is a masculine perversion. It begins with the little boy turning away from the evidence of anatomical difference disclosed by his mother's naked body, by her different and apparently mutilated genitalia (so the theory goes). Faced with the implied threat to his own penis, the boy undergoes a psychic splitting. In the fetishist, this defensive gesture later becomes fixed as perversion. The subject attempts to soothe and to pleasure himself by ritually deploying a substitute for the lost object. The fetishist, however, stops short of humor, of adopting a parental attitude toward the helpless ego. Instead, he comforts himself with the piece of fur or the shoe that marks the last moment in which he believed in the existence of the mother's penis, and he tortures himself with these souvenirs of loss, haunted by the threat of castration.

In maternal fetishism—which Freud fails to theorize but which has become a significant extension of fetish theory in psychoanalytic feminism—the mother mothers herself against her own dread of loss by fetishizing items of clothing and other mementoes of the child's infancy. Like the male fetishist, the maternal fetishist, infantilized by the trauma of loss, suffers and derives pleasure from inflating that loss to tragic proportions. The artist Mary Kelly in particular has represented and analyzed the process by which maternity is perverted into a fetishistic scene under the pressure of patriarchal law (the same law that gives rise to the male fetishist's perverse defense). Kelly's *Post-Partum Document* (1973-1979) describes maternal fetishism not as an aberration in mothering, but as a condition of maternal experience under patriarchy.[3]

Blind to the relation between fetishism, femininity, and maternity, as well as to fetishism's cultural pervasion, Freud nevertheless puts his finger on fetishism's lack: it lacks a feeling for fun. For Freud, fetishistic splitting is pathological, while humorous splitting is adaptive. Humor is the inverse of fetishism; or, to put it another way, humor might offer a way around fetishism.

In Freud's writings, humor and jokes are empowering, even curative. In *Jokes and Their Relation to the Unconscious* (1905), Freud argues that because the origin of jokes, like dreams, lies in the unconscious, jokes carry the explosive intensity of anxiety, frustration, and desire, but also the power symbolically to recast such feelings. Jokes also resist external authority. As Freud points out, even a poor caricature provokes laughter "because we count rebellion against authority a merit."[4] Certainly Freud did, and his study explores in compulsive depth and detail the ways in which jokes "make aggressiveness or criticism possible against persons in exalted positions who claim to exercise authority."[5] And if jokes serve to undermine hierarchy,

---

[3] Mary Kelly, *Post-Partum Document* (London: Routledge and Kegan Paul, 1983).
[4] S. Freud, *Jokes and Their Relation to the Unconscious, SE VIII*, 105.
[5] Ibid.

Freud argues, the comic gesture in particular promotes "the discharge of a difference."[6] Recalling the child's preoccupation with comparison—with what is greater or smaller, stronger or weaker than itself—Freud contends that the comic gesture rebels against the constraints of an inferior position and has its origins in "an infantile point of view."[7] Slapstick, for example, recalls the infantile experience of helplessness in which, lacking mastery of its own body, the child misjudges balance and proportion—staggers, slips, misses, and falls. Taking on the role of the child and making fun of physical failure, the comedian, in effect, turns infantile humiliation into an excuse for pleasure.

While jokes and comic gestures produce pleasure by discharging difference, fetishism takes pleasure in refusing difference, instituting a personal sexual ritual over which the fetishist exercises complete control. This may in part explain why fetishism is funny, without being playful. For we all recognize the child's exclusion from adult sexual arrangements, and can appreciate the wish to devise a perverse alternative. Similarly, we can all sympathize with the mother's desire to hold onto her baby and her maternal power. Maternal fetishism, after all, recalls the wish to cling to our own mothers, or even to our infant selves, to a time "when we had no need of humor to make us feel happy in our life." Fetishism is defined precisely by an "ignorance of the comic," by a defiant belief in the possibility of a humorless happiness.

Fetishism is funny, but it fails as humor. Fetishism has in common with jokes a defiance of authority, and it shares with the comic gesture an insistent return to an infantile point of view. Like the comic scenario, fetishism is a defense against the degradations of childhood. It therefore contains the rudiments of comedy—an infantile point of view, childish humiliation, the tone of despair that attaches to early frustrations, and a rebellious repudiation of rules—but fails to turn them to comic purpose. For this would require the fetishist to nod to reality, while laughing in its face. Humor, by contrast, seizes on reality in order to transcend it. It masters anxiety and contests external authority in a more high-minded, or high-handed, way than the joke. For humor relieves anxiety by asserting control, the superego turning loss into a mere pretext for ego pleasure. When we lose ourselves in laughter, Freud suggests, we are really losing our loss, mastering our disappointments, frustrations, and anxieties. And the profoundest form of this knowing laughter, humor, is, somewhat surprisingly, the work of the parental superego, of prohibition itself.[8]

---

[6] Ibid., 221.

[7] Ibid., 226.

[8] As Suleiman observes, "Freud emphasizes the liberating function of humor and contrasts it to mere jokes, humor possessing, according to him, 'grandeur,' and 'dignity,' whereas jokes ... do not." See "Playing and Motherhood," 279.

1. It's a conversion toward another kind of energy

From the beginning of his work toward a theory of psychoanalysis, Freud exploited the effects of humor. As early as *Studies on Hysteria* (1895), he identified a punning logic in neurotic symptoms, and found those patients with a well-developed sense of humor most susceptible to improvement. One patient, Frau Cäcilie M., for example, obtained relief from her psychical pain by laughing aloud at her own hysterical puns. Reporting, for instance, that she once suffered a sudden excruciating heachache while lying in bed under the watchful eye of her grandmother, who gave her a "piercing" look, the patient suddenly "broke out in a loud laugh, and the pain once more disappeared."[9]

Perhaps the most sustained artistic analysis of the structural relation between fetishism and humor is to be found in the work of Louise Bourgeois (b. 1911). In the mid 1930s, Bourgeois traveled in Surrealist circles in Paris, residing in the very rue de Seine building that housed the Surrealist gallery Gradiva. Then, in 1938, she moved to New York, soon to be joined by an exiled community of artists and intellectuals in flight from the German occupation. There, she became an articulate critic of Surrealism, the movement she had encountered as an art student, and which delivered her first, stinging professional rejection.[10] By the artist's own account, her work of the 1940s and beyond was devoted to staging a "rebuttal" to Surrealism.[11]

That this rebuttal to Surrealism begins with the fetish is not surprising. For the Surrealist preoccupation with fetishism is matched only by its fascination with hysteria. Surrealist art embraced fetishism as a form of resistance to bourgeois morality and a means to liberate unconscious desire. The fetishist's rejection of conventional sexuality and external authority enabled the Surrealists to turn the Freudian account of fetishism to artistic and political purpose. Bourgeois's work, however, exposes the political weakness of fetishism in its Surrealist representation: combining anxiety and sexuality, Surrealist fetishism effectively validates male sexual insecurity. It dramatizes, even celebrates, the male subject's fear of, and fascination with, the female body, often to violent or degrading effect. It is sometimes funny, but not humorous.

[9]   Freud, "Fräulein Elisabeth von R.," in Joseph Breuer and Sigmund Freud, *Studies on Hysteria*, trans. James and Alix Strachey, ed. James Strachey, Alix Strachey, and Angela Richards (London: Penguin, 1974), 253.

[10]   For André Breton and Marcel Duchamp, she was, she has said, "just a girl, and women were not to be taken seriously anyway." Although Bourgeois, with her perfect English, became a valued intermediary for the new arrivals, for her "it was the Left Bank again, and although I was now close to them, I objected to them violently. They were so lordly and pontifical." Bourgeois's remarks are quoted in Barbara Rose, "Race, Sex, and Louise Bourgeois," *Vogue*, September 1987, 168; and in Paul Gardner, *Louise Bourgeois* (New York: Universe Books, 1993), 26.

[11]   Louise Bourgeois, interviewed by the author, 27 February 1996.

In 1947, Bourgeois produced a series of paintings on the theme of the *femme-maison*, or woman-house. Punning on the English word *housewife*, the *femme-maison* motif conflates the female body with an architectural façade. Stacked like the stories of a building, its concatenation of parts mimics the stylistic discontinuity of Surrealist composition. In particular, the *femme-maison* parodies the exquisite corpse—that quintessential Surrealist mode of collective production in which disparate elements are conjoined. With a joke's economy of means, the *femme-maison* combines several roles Surrealism assigns to women—femme fatale, hysteric, female muse, phallic mother.[12]

The theme of the female body caged, of the head masked and muted, however also caricatures Surrealist representations of the female body as fetish. Compare, for example, the *femme-maison* to André Masson's *Mannequin*, with head in birdcage, made for the Surrealist Exhibition of 1938, and displayed in a row of similar figures—styled by Max Ernst, Jean Arp, Marcel Duchamp, Salvador Dalí, and Joan Miró, among others—that outlined the exhibition's Surrealist Street.[13] The figure's sex marked by a bikini bottom beaded with glass eyes and crowned with feathers, Masson's *Mannequin* is a caricature of a fetishistic representation of the female body: an object or item of clothing associated with the genitalia becomes the focus of desire. The figure of the *femme-maison* in turn caricatures this caricature, and in the process significantly improves on the original joke. For in contrast to the lifeless *Mannequin*'s frozen pose, the *femme-maison* is animated and elastic: the legs spread and the vaginal lips part to form the perfect outline of a comic-book smile.

One picture shows three arms hailing from the windows of a brownstone row house, a typical New York building style. Below the stairs, this three-armed figure's elastic legs spring apart, opening the sex. In a second painting, a voluptuous figure stands nymph-like, submerged in water, a pedimented building to helmet her head. Highlighted and circled, the figure's cleft sex pops out as a graffito-like hole in the picture. Parodying *Mannequin*'s rendering of the female body as catatonic and gagged, the *femme-maison* is styled as a cartoon character. Bourgeois seizes on this as a form by which to invert the fetish. Nude from the waist down, sex exposed, her body trapped in a house, this is no empty *caricature* but a *character* whose travails we follow from frame to frame as she struggles to break free of her encumbrance.

[12] The *femme-maison* paintings have been widely reproduced in catalogues. See Deborah Wye, *Louise Bourgeois* (New York: Museum of Modern Art, 1982), 44-5.

[13] See William S. Rubin, *Dada, Surrealism, and Their Heritage* (New York: Museum of Modern Art, 1968), 153.

Figure 1. *Femme-Maison*, 1946-47.
Oil and ink on linen - 91.4 x 35.5 cm
Collection John D. Kahlbetzer.
Photo: Inge Morath
Courtesy of the artist.

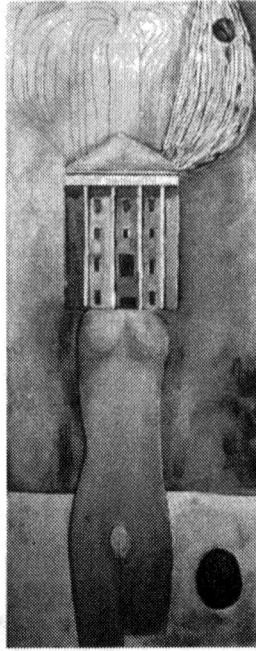

Figure 2. *Femme-Maison*, 1946-47.
Oil and ink on linen - 91.4 x 35.5 cm
Photo: Donald Greenhaus
Courtesy of the artist.

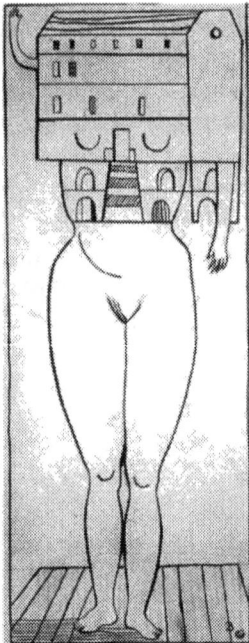

Figure 3. *Femme-Maison*, 1947. Ink on paper - 23.1 x 9.2 cm
Collection Solomon R. Guggenheim Meuseum, New York.
Photo: Eeeva Inkeri. Courtesy of the artist.

The aggression latent in the fetish for female subjects is a powerful theme in Bourgeois's art, one to which she turns with her earliest sculptures, the Personages. First shown in an installation of seventeen wood figures at the Peridot Gallery in New York in 1949, the Personages were slender posts, beams, and planks of balsa wood, painted black, white, or red and scaled to the human body. The figures were set directly on the floor, without bases, and arranged in pairs and clusters around the gallery. According to Bourgeois, these tapered poles scaled to the human body stood as "a kind of memorial" for family members left behind in France during the war years.[14] She has referred to one piece, for example, as "a portable brother—a pole you could carry around."[15] Described by one reviewer as "superficially reminiscent of African and Oceanic fetishes," the Personages elicited suggestions from another of "a primitive mood" and "a disturbed spirit at work."[16] Gathered in the stage-like setting of the gallery, they appeared to stand "ready for use in some primitive rite."[17] And indeed it is clear that the Personages summon an association with the primitive that is a deeply ingrained feature of Surrealist sculpture. As with the *femme-maison*, however, the Personage was a figure through which to critique and recast a Surrealist trope, in this case, the tribal fetish.

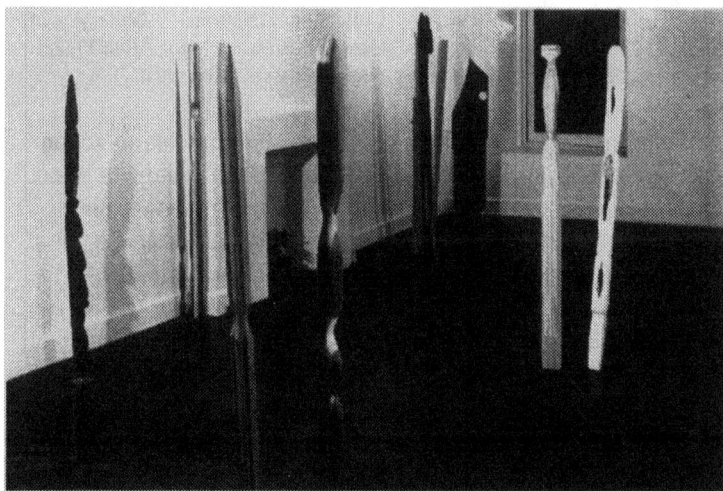

Figure 4. Installation view of solo exhibition, Peridot Gallery, New York, 1950. Photo: Aaron Siskind. Courtesy of the artist.

[14] Quoted in Robert Storr, interview, *Galeries Magazine* (Paris), June-July 1990, 100.

[15] Quoted in Lucy Lippard, "Louise Bourgeois: From the Inside Out," in *From the Center: Feminist Essays on Women's Art* (New York: E.P. Dutton & Co., 1976), 240.

[16] M.G., exhibition review, Peridot Gallery, *Art News*, vol. 48 (October 1949), 46; P[esella] L[evy], exhibition review, Peridot Gallery, *Art Digest*, vol. 25 (1 October 1950), 16.

[17] Levy, review, 16.

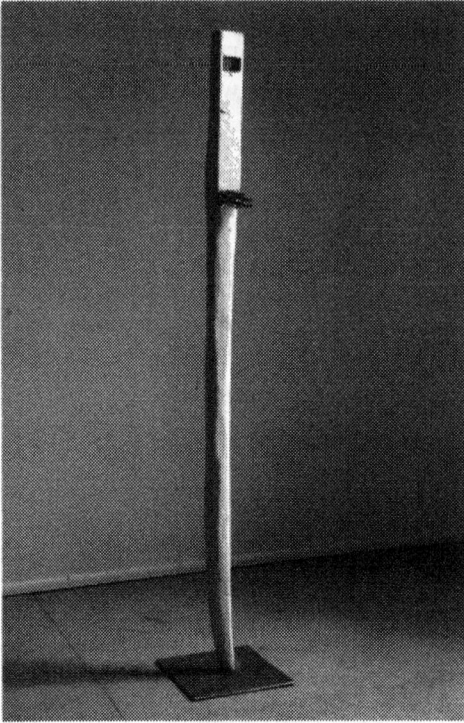

Figure 5. *Portrait of C.Y.*, 1947-49. Painted wood and nails. 169.5 x 30.4 x 30.4 cm. Collection National Gallery of Canada, Ottawa. Photo: Allan Finkelman. Courtesy of the artist.

The placement of the figures directly on the floor and in relation to one another and to the room was also, according to the artist, a statement about their reality. For it was, Bourgeois says, her dissatisfaction with painting's "level of reality" that prompted her turn to sculpture, convinced that she could express "much deeper things in three dimensions."[18] Displaced from the virtual space of the pedestal, to which sculpture is conventionally consigned, the Personages required, according to Bourgeois, "the room, the six sides of the cube" in which to exist, and occupied "a social space."[19] They belonged, that is, to a territory shared by viewers, akin to a place of ritual. The "primitive rite" the figures celebrated was, in simplest terms, the cultural ritual of the gallery itself.

One figure, *Portrait of C.Y.*, is a square post, five and a half feet tall, painted white, and punctuated by three acts of cutting: the top is pierced by a rectangular slot; a cluster of nails is driven into the shaft at a level corresponding roughly to the mouth or heart; and the corners of the post are filed and honed from the midsection downward to the sharpened lower tip.

18 Quoted in Wye, *Louise Bourgeois*, 18; and in Wye, "A Drama of the Self: Louise Bourgeois as Printmaker," in Wye and Carol Smith, *The Prints of Louise Bourgeois* (New York: Museum of Modern Art, 1994), 23.

19 Quoted in Wye, *Louise Bourgeois*, 18; Susi Bloch, "An Interview with Louise Bourgeois," *Art Journal*, vol. 35, no. 4 (Summer 1976), 372.

The piece is precariously balanced, poised on a narrow point that gives the figure a stake-like sharpness. That the nails driven into the post are metonyms of this lancet shape makes *Portrait of C.Y.* both the object of aggression and the aggressive object. "Its identity as a fetish object," the curator and critic Deborah Wye has observed, "revealed by nails aggressively piercing it, is unmistakable."[20] This is Bourgeois's retrospective description of the piece:

> This refers to a real person.... . She was a houseguest of mine in Easton [Connecticut, USA] when I had three children. She wanted my attention all day. Her presence was exhausting to me. Whenever I prepared a meal, she said, "No thank you, I'm not hungry." So, she irritated me. This piece kept me from doing to her what I did to the sculpture. It's a conversion toward another kind of energy. It kept me from being objectionable.[21]

Elaborating on Bourgeois's own account of the figure as enacting her revenge on an irritating houseguest, Jeremy Strick has suggested that "the nails Bourgeois hammered into the head of this figure allowed the artist to exorcise her anger, while also perhaps serving a function akin to sticking pins in voodoo dolls."[22] One effect of this gesture—which must be understood as a humorous device, and a partly self-mocking one—is to lay claim to the aggressive act in the making of art. Bourgeois's vivid description of a domestic scene in which she plays the role of host and mother alludes to depths of aggression ("primitive" violence) in everyday feminine experience. Here, the fetish stands in for the object to prevent aggression from becoming act, but also, as work of sculpture by a "woman artist" in the late 1940s, to *facilitate* aggression becoming act.[23]

In this connection, I would like to propose a comparison, this time not with a Surrealist work, but with a much earlier literary text by a woman writer: namely, George Eliot's *The Mill on the Floss* (1860). For, a fetish that bears a notable resemblance to *Portrait of C.Y.* is the one that the novel's protagonist, Maggie Tulliver, contrives to contain and sustain her aggression, "a Fetish which she punished for all her misfortunes":

> This was the trunk of a large wooden doll, which once stared with the roundest of eyes above the reddest of cheeks: but was now entirely defaced by a long career of vicarious suffering. Three nails driven into the head commemorated as many crises in Maggie's nine years of earthly struggle; that luxury of vengeance having been suggested to her by the picture of Jael destroying Sisera

20 Wye, *Louise Bourgeois*, 19.
21 Quoted in Jeremy Strick, *Louise Bourgeois: The Personages* (Saint Louis: Saint Louis Art Museum, 1994), 23.
22 Ibid., p. 24.
23 For a fuller, illustrated discussion of this work, see my "'Fantastic Reality': A Note on Louise Bourgeois's *Portrait of C.Y.*," *Sculpture Journal* vol. 5 (2001).

in the old Bible. The last nail had been driven in with a fiercer stoke than usual, for the Fetish had on that occasion represented aunt Glegg.[24]

Scorned for her refusal to emulate conventional feminine behavior, to curb her temper, comb her hair, and keep herself tidy, Maggie vents her fury on the Fetish, then soothes herself "by alternately grinding and beating the wooden head" of the doll. For Maggie, the Fetish performs its orthodox function as a doll—a support for femininity—only in absorbing aggression (keeping the offending Aunt Glegg safe from abuse). Its more obvious function, like *Portrait of C.Y.*, however is to register aggression, to claim it.

Maggie Tulliver's emotional vigor, in combination with her prodigious intelligence, creates a sense of foreboding even before the novel's tragic events are set in train. In *The Mill on the Floss*, affective intensity in a woman tests the social order: the more Maggie's vitality is suppressed, the more subversive becomes its effects—a model of femininity as excess that can be related to the account of hysteria Freud was shortly to develop. For in the female hysteric as described by Freud (and later claimed as the Surrealist muse), excessive affect is a subversive force. Upon his discovery of the Oedipus complex, Freud would trace hysterical excess to a sexual point of origin, retrospectively reading hysteria as the manifestation of an unconscious conflict between desire and prohibition. In this account, hysteria arises from a clash between desire for the father, or a father figure, and the incest taboo. Yet, an aggressive trend strains beneath the surface of Freud's earlier case studies, suggesting that hysteria might also have been theorized as an ambivalence of aggression.

In his account of the case of Frau Cäcilie M., for example, whose punning symptoms I have already mentioned, Freud reports that the patient's painful emotional experiences were "accompanied by a stabbing sensation in the region of the heart" and at other time by pain like "nails being driven into the head."[25] He traces her hysteria, the most distressing symptom of which is violent facial neuralgia, to unanswered insults. At this time, Freud was still using hypnosis to treat his patients and noted that, under its effect, Frau Cäcilie M. "saw herself back in a period of great mental irritability toward her husband. She described a conversation which she had had with him and a remark of his which she had felt as a bitter insult. Suddenly she put her hand to her cheek, gave a loud cry of pain and said: 'It was like a slap in the face.' With this her pain and her attack were both at an end."[26]

Frau Cäcilie M.'s revelation is that resentment of her husband's insults, and a cultural prohibition on her rebuttal, have, in effect, trapped psyche in soma, resulting in a punning corporeal symptom. *Conversion* is Freud's

---

[24] George Eliot, *The Mill on the Floss* (London: Everyman, 1996), 22.
[25] Freud, *Studies on Hysteria*, 253.
[26] Ibid., 251.

technical term for the mechanism by which a psychical conflict manifests itself as a physical symptom. His theory of hysteria centers on the repression of sexual desire, so Freud focuses on the conversion of libidinal impulses into symptoms that prevent those wishes from being felt: in place of sexual fantasies, the patient experiences painful sensations that block them. In his account of the treatment of Frau Cäcilie M., however, Freud concentrates not on sexual impulses, but on aggressive ones. He traces the patient's hysteria to a series of episodes, beginning in adolescence, when insulting remarks were directed to her and she was unable to make any reply. Forced to "swallow" these insults rather than answer them, Frau Cäcilie M. converted the offending speech into a physical sensation. "In taking an expression literally," Freud observes, "and in feeling the 'stab in the heart' or the 'slap in the face' after some slighting remark as a real event, the hysteric is not taking liberties with words but is simply reviving once more the sensation to which the verbal expression owes its justification."[27]

For Freud, hysteria is "primitive" in that it ("rightly") restores "the original meaning of the words" for which language has substituted "a figurative picture."[28] Conducted before the talking cure was fully formulated as a technique, Freud's brief account of the treatment of Frau Cäcilie M. centers on an inhibition not of sexual impulses, but of precisely that form of speech Louise Bourgeois would later use to describe her relation to Surrealism: namely, rebuttal. And it is Freud, in *Jokes and Their Relation to the Unconscious*, who provides a particularly apt description of the technique of rebuttal that Bourgeois employs in her early works. An effective rejoinder, he explains, depends on the skill of the offended party in turning an insult back on the aggressor. An insult made in the form of a joke can, Freud contends, be "safely avenged" by taking up the allusion and returning it, but the effectiveness of the rejoinder is an index of the victim's dexterity in picking up and improving on the original joke.[29]

2. The woman turns into a blade

Beginning in the 1960s, Louise Bourgeois radically transformed her sculptural practice, turning from upright figures to bodily objects in plaster, latex, and carved marble. One such work is *Femme Couteau* (Knife Woman, 1969), "a wrapped and folded marble blade with delicate pudenda exposed," in Lucy Lippard's evocative description.[30] A smooth, narrow, polished object suggestive of a clitoris, *Femme Couteau* recalls a well-known Surrealist

---

[27] Ibid., 254.
[28] Ibid.
[29] Freud, *Jokes*, 104.
[30] Lippard, "From the Inside Out," 246.

sculpture, Giacometti's *Disagreeable Object* of 1931, a wood "objet sans base" in the form of a penis with a spiked tip. *Femme Couteau* explicitly counterposes a representation of female genitalia to this Surrealist work, in which Freudian fetishism and tribal fetishism are combined. In the context of Bourgeois's self-proclaimed rebuttal to Surrealism, it is useful to consider what *Femme Couteau* suggests about that other work, and about the Surrealist discourse of fetishism.

Of *Disagreeable Object*, Hal Foster has noted, aggressivity is joined with desire, "the narcissistically disagreeable (the castrative) with the perversely desirable (the fetishistic)."[31] Or, as Michael Brenson observed of this work in 1974, aggressivity is the counterpoint to infantile anxiety: "one end is vulnerable and helpless, the other end is aggressive and menacing." Giacometti's tusk- or club-like object, fitted with finger grooves and a pricked tip resembles, according to Brenson, an embryo: "The round section is the head, the two concavities, the eyes, and the tusk-like section the body. On the back of the body is a spine. On the back of the head are four grooves. If the viewer places his hand so that four of his fingers are in the grooves, he will be holding the work in a cradling or rocking position."[32] These readings focus specifically on *Disagreeable Object*'s significance for the male subject, which is, after all, Surrealism's concern. The castrative threat of the spiked phallic weapon however is also menacing for the female subject, or viewer—without any compensatory protective or narcissistic effect. Indeed, *Disagreeable Object* might well be seen as an object that encapsulates male and female genital anxiety, while functioning defensively—as a fetish—only for the male subject.

The female fetishist, for Freud, is an impossible pervert: the woman is unable to fear the loss of what instead she simply lacks. *Femme Couteau* however invokes—through its polished surface, its prop-like size, its conjuncture of round and sharp, and its implied solicitation of the viewer's touch—a female fetishism in a Surrealist form. The work can be viewed as the inverse of *Disagreeable Object*, encapsulating male and female mutilation anxiety but functioning as a fetish only for the female subject. *Femme Couteau*, however, is not only a female fetish. While it demonstrates what the logic of a female fetish might be, this work also points to other aporias, other blind spots, in the phallocentric sexual theories of psychoanalysis.

---

[31] Hal Foster, *Compulsive Beauty* (Cambridge: MIT Press, 1993), 93.
[32] Michael Francis Brenson, "The Early Work of Giacometti, 1925-1935" (Ph.D. diss., The Johns Hopkins University, 1974), 117-8.

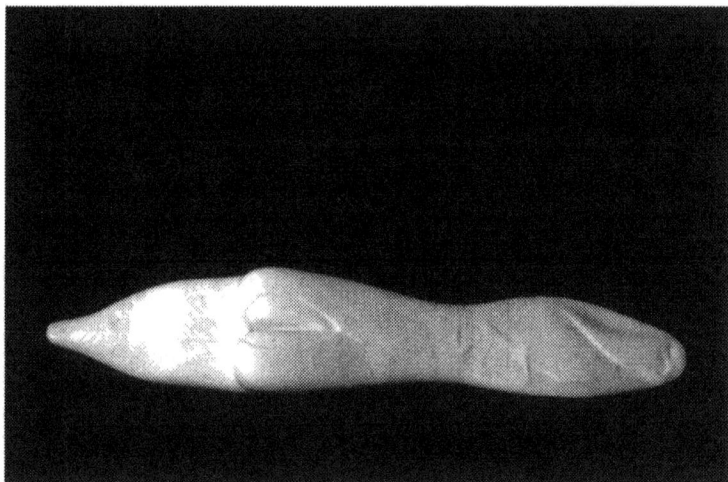

Figure 6. *Femme-Couteau*, 1969-70. Carved pink marble. 8.8 x 66.9 x 12.3 cm.
Emily and Jerry Spiegel Family Collection. Photo: Allan Finkelman.
Courtesy of the artist.

Freud theorized the fear of genital mutilation as castration anxiety. Bourgeois, echoing later psychoanalytic reflections on the subject, has suggested that such fears are presexual and pregendered in origin, and give rise to fantasies of aggression, of using one's own body as a weapon. As the artist once remarked of *Femme Couteau*, "the woman turns into a blade"; then, in the next breath, she added that the woman might revert to a girl who "feels vulnerable because she can be wounded by the penis" and so "tries to take on the weapon of the aggressor." This anxiety, which encompasses not only the fear of physical harm but also the fear of one's own aggression ("when one becomes aggressive, she becomes terribly afraid"), arises, according to Bourgeois, "at the terror level which precedes anything sexual."[33]

The female genitalia play a minor part in Freud's account of sexuality. Male castration anxiety and female penis envy overshadow any separate significance the female genitalia might hold. Nevertheless, in psychoanalytic discourse of the 1920s and 1930s (and so contemporaneous with Surrealism), female castration anxiety was a leading topic, debated by, among others, Karl Abraham, Helene Deutsch, Karen Horney, and Melanie Klein. A recurrent theme in this literature is the woman's dissatisfaction with female genitalia as a cause of neurosis (penis envy, the female castration complex, frigidity, and more). Abraham, for example, suggests that "the female genitalia is looked

---

[33] Quoted in Seiberling, "The Female View of Erotica," *New York*, vol. 7, February 11, 1974; quoted in Lippard, "From the Inside Out," 246.

upon as a *wound*, and as such it represents an effect of castration."[34] By the logic of inversion, however, the wound might become a blade. Abraham develops this point in a somewhat unexpected manner, claiming, "I know several cases in which women after being deflorated had an outburst of affect and hit or throttled their husband."[35] Abraham's next assertion may be categorical—"There is no mistaking the significance of such conduct: the woman revenges herself for the injury done to her physical integrity"—but there is no doubt something to it.[36] At least he takes seriously the culturally sensitive question of female aggression, a topic that would figure prominently in the work of his protégé Melanie Klein.

In her early work in the field of child analysis, Klein attempted to discover what castration anxieties, or genital anxieties, children might actually demonstrate through their play. Her observations and interpretations are informed by contemporary debates on female castration anxiety (she, too, assumes that the girl interprets her "lack of a penis" as a grievance or punishment).[37] Klein, however, sees castration, for children of both sexes, as arising from early experiences of frustration, the loss of the breast in weaning primary among them. To fantasies of aggression and retribution—such as the fear of being punished for attacks on the breast, the insides of the mother's body, or the father's penis—the child adds the fear of genital mutilation. In an early paper, "Psychological Principles of Child Analysis" (1926), Klein describes the case of a little girl, Rita, who was brought for analysis at the age of two years and nine months. Klein detects in Rita's aversion to games anxious feelings of guilt about her own aggressive fantasies. Rita avoids playing with dolls because, according to Klein, she does not "*dare* to play at being a mother." Having fantasied attacks on her own mother's insides when her mother was pregnant, and against the baby itself when it appeared, Rita perceives a doll as both a reproach and a threat, encapsulating her own aggression and the potential for violent retribution on the part of the damaged "internal mother." Before going to sleep at night, Klein reports, Rita "insisted on being tightly rolled up in the bedclothes for fear that 'a mouse or butty might come through the window and bite off her butty (genital).'"[38] When preparing for sleep, Rita demands a covering for her body that is reminiscent of the swaddling clothes in which small infants are wrapped to soothe them— a demand that recalls, perhaps, the fear of penetration that, as Juliet Mitchell

---

[34] Karl Abraham, "Manifestations of the Female Castration Complex" (1920), in *Karl Abraham: Selected Papers on Psychoanalysis*, trans. Douglas Bryan and Alix Strachey (London: Maresfield Library, 1927; reprint, 1988), 340.

[35] Ibid., 345.

[36] Ibid., 345-6.

[37] Melanie Klein, "Early Stages of the Oedipus Conflict" (1928), in *The Selected Melanie Klein*, ed. Juliet Mitchell (New York: Free Press, 1986), 77.

[38] Klein, "The Psychological Principles of Infant Analysis" (1926), in *The Selected Melanie Klein, op.cit.*, 62.

has argued, may be the very model of all traumatic experience.[39] In effect, Rita turns her body into a butty, wrapped and enfolded, as Lippard describes the *Femme Couteau*.

Femme Couteau offers a representation of female genitalia as the object of narcissistic affection and solicitous concern, but also the object of anxiety and aggression for the female subject herself. It also suggests that the very possibility of thinking about female sexuality is compromised by the absence of such representations. Freud, for example, contends that for the child entering the genital stage, only one genital, "namely the male one, comes into account": "What is present, therefore, is not a primacy of the genitals, but a primacy of the *phallus*." And the opposite of the phallus is castration: "The antithesis here is between having *a male genital* and being *castrated*. It is not until development has reached its completion at puberty that the sexual polarity coincides with *male* and *female*."[40] For little boys, even at this stage of intensive sexual research, Freud contends "the female genitals never seem to be discovered."[41]

For Freud, it is only in infantile sexuality that the female genitalia do not come into account, and that sexual difference is construed according to the either/or of phallic/castrated: adult sexuality (fetishism aside) recasts sexual difference in terms of male and female.[42] The feminist theorist Jane Gallop however has suggested a different reading of Freud's theories, arguing that "it remains an open question whether there exists any adult sexuality, whether there is any masculinity that is beyond the phallic phase, that does not need to equate femininity with castration."[43] What if fetishism is but one variation on the "infantile point of view" of masculine sexuality? What if adult sexuality is based not on sexual difference, but on a fetishistic phallus fixation?

---

[39] Juliet Mitchell, *Mad Men and Medusas: Reclaiming Hysteria and the Effects of Sibling Relations on the Human Condition* (London: Penguin, 2000), 138.

[40] Freud, "The Infantile Genital Organization (An Interpretation into the Theory of Sexuality)" (1923), in *On Sexuality: Three Essays on the Theory of Sexuality and Other Works*, trans. James Strachey, ed. Angela Richards (London: Penguin, 1991), 309.

[41] Ibid., 311.

[42] Even then, however, the female genital that is discovered is the vagina: "The vagina is now valued as a place of shelter for the penis; it enters into the heritage of the womb" (312). The clitoris, in Freud's account, does not belong to adult sexuality, but to the phallic phase, in which "the female genitals never seem to be discovered" by the boy child.

[43] Jane Gallop, "Beyond the Phallus," in *Thinking Through the Body* (New York: Columbia University Press, 1988), 125.

3. The baby-wish simply takes the place of the penis-wish

Fillette (1968) is a two-foot long latex phallus. Bourgeois deploys it as a prop in a 1982 portrait by Robert Mapplethorpe. There, the seventy-year-old artist, wearing a tufted coat of monkey fur, grins broadly, a smile reported again and again in the widening crinkles of her face. Under her right arm she clasps the phallus. As her fingers firmly grasp the tip, behind her elbow nestle the big, shiny balls. The coarse, bumpy skin of the tip pushes through the V-shaped opening of a sleeve fitted over the shaft, the ridges formed by its raised seam mimicking the veins that run across Bourgeois's flexed hand below. Staged in the year of Bourgeois's 1982 retrospective at the Museum of Modern Art in New York, the photographic session with Mapplethorpe, which was intended to produce a portrait for the show's catalogue, resulted in a tongue-in-cheek image of the phallus-wielding woman artist in the guise of a fetishist. It is with this work, and Bourgeois's demonstration of it in her poses with Mapplethorpe, that I would like to return once more to the question: what's so funny about fetishism?[44]

Strung up on a hook, as it is displayed in exhibition, *Fillette* appears castrated (but also phallic), "a big, suspended, decaying phallus, definitely on the rough side," as Lawrence Alloway once observed.[45] Bourgeois sees it differently, claiming, "You can carry it around like a baby, have it as a doll."[46] In 1982, the artist enacted this claim, posing with *Fillette* as a prop in the session with Mapplethorpe. On the day appointed to visit the photographer's studio, Bourgeois anticipated, she says, "a catastrophe," and prepared for the event by looking around the house for props that might be employed as "supports" to allay her anxiety.[47] She selected two, a shaggy coat and *Fillette*, a work made fourteen years earlier but that was at the time "hanging among others."[48] "I knew," she says, "that I would get comfort from holding and rocking the piece."[49] Here Bourgeois plays the fetishist's game, purporting to calm her anxiety with an outsized phallus and a cloak of fur. In some of Mapplethorpe's shots, the artist clasps the sculpture tightly under her elbow like a pet phallus. In other poses, supported from its underside, nestled against

---

[44] For a history of the Mapplethorpe series and images of the contact sheets from the session, which I discuss below, see my "Pretty as a Picture: Louise Bourgeois's *Fillette*," *Parkett* 27 (1991).

[45] Lawrence Alloway, "Art," *The Nation*, March 27, 1972; quoted in Wye, *Louise Bourgeois*, 27.

[46] Bourgeois, quoted in Lippard, "From the Inside Out," 243.

[47] Bourgeois, interview with the author, August 23, 1993.

[48] Ibid.

[49] Quoted from a statement by Bourgeois on August 19, 1990 at the Medal Day ceremony of the MacDowell Colony, published in *MacDowell Colony News*, vol. 20, no. 1 (Spring 1991).

the body—fastened to the hip or snuggled to the breast—*Fillette* does however look very much the baby.

Mapplethorpe's contact sheets show Bourgeois cradling the object against her hip like an infant to be patted and stroked; cupping in her hands the balls that, with the sculpture upended and turned to face the camera, suddenly read as plump, foreshortened infant legs; gazing tenderly down on the tip transformed to a tiny head arched back and fastened to a neck, the sculpture's shaft, that pokes up out of the collar of some little dress or blanket. Or, resting horizontally against the artist's breast, *Fillette* seems to relax open-mouthed in sleep, tended by a soothing hand, its head comfortably settled in the crook of an arm. And then again, pinned rigidly in place, an elbow and a clenched hand securing it to Bourgeois's hip, the body seems to yank back, the back to arch, the little thing frantically straining to free itself as the pressure of a fist or a gripped hand tightens against its every exertion, only to loosen suddenly, casually tucking the agitated, spent body under an arm and carrying it off.

Bourgeois here parodies a truism of Freudian theory, the equation penis=baby that secures the female subject, via the role of mother, a place within a phallocentric economy of desire. She shows that the structure of this normative femininity, in which the female subject turns to the baby as a phallic substitute, can also be seen as structurally similar to fetishism. As Rachel Bowlby succinctly explains, "the baby-wish simply takes the place of the penis-wish: it is the substitute and it is also what hides its continuing existence."[50] Seen this way, femininity in the Freudian scheme parallels the quintessentially masculine perversion of fetishism. For the contradiction in which the baby serves simultaneously to allay and to deny the woman's disappointment about the loss of the wished-for penis produces a split subject (the mother) who, like the fetishist, can relieve her anxiety only by fixating on the very object that embodies it, in this case the baby.

Bourgeois's poses with *Fillette* enact and caricature the phallus=baby equation while offering a comic demonstration of the resemblance between fetishism and femininity as described by Freud. Her performance plays this chain of displacements as farce, imputing to the scenarios of fetishism and femininity an almost slapstick improbability. Feminine sexuality under patriarchy, her poses suggest, is necessarily contrived—as contrived as the sexual rituals of the fetishist. Bourgeois's performance also peels away the sentimentality that adheres to motherhood's cultural reputation, laying bare a repressed maternal aggression. In her play between protective and sadistic impulses toward both phallus and baby, fetishism and mothering are brought together, but this conjuncture is not enacted through the clinging and humorless practice of maternal fetishism. When Bourgeois mothers *Fillette*, she pokes fun at the mother's syrupy, lustrous gaze and dread of loss.

---

[50] Rachel Bowlby, "Still Crazy after All These Years," in *Between Feminism and Psychoanalysis*, ed. Teresa Brennan (New York: Routledge, 1989), 50.

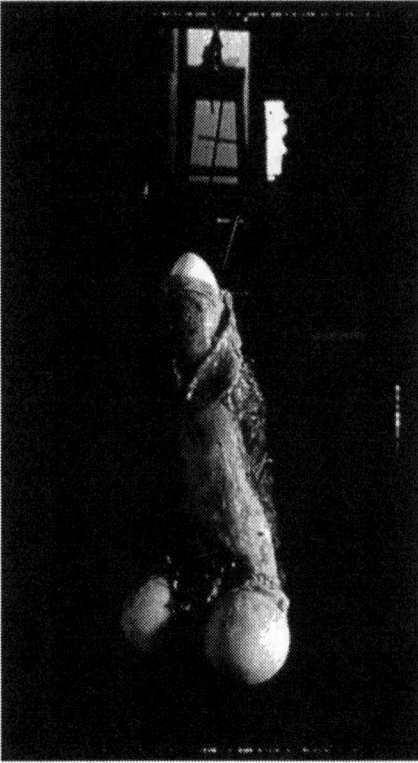

Figure 7. *Filette*, 1968. Latex over plaster. 59.6 x 26.6 x 19.6 cm. Collection Museum of Modern Art, New York. Photo C by Peter Moore. Courtesy of the artist.

Parodying the maternal fixation on the baby, Bourgeois's poses replace the good, or good enough, patriarchal mother—her role fulfilled in the possession and nurturing of a little one—with the bad enough mother, a playful, aggressive subject.[51] This play with fetishism and maternity is performed under the sign of humor, eliciting laughter in relation to two notoriously humorless practices. So it is through a comic misreading that Bourgeois's poses with *Fillette* associate fetishism, perversely, with femininity and humor.

The picture that was actually used as the frontispiece of the catalogue for Bourgeois's 1982 Museum of Modern Art retrospective was a cropped version of the now-famous Mapplethorpe portrait, reduced to a head shot. This excision of *Fillette* from the photograph, displacing the grin from its gag,

[51]   The "good enough mother" is the celebrated formulation of D.W. Winnicott. As Janice Doane and Devon Hodges have noted, while Winnicott apparently "empowers the mother by acknowledging her subjectivity and her work as nurturer," he simultaneously constructs mothers as "objects for the regulatory discourse of experts." Doane and Hodges, *From Klein to Kristeva: Psychoanalytic Feminism and the Search for the "Good Enough" Mother* (Ann Arbor: University of Michigan Press, 1992), p. 21. For more on the subversive potential of the mother in recent feminist art, including that of Louise Bourgeois, see my "Bad Enough Mother," *October* 71 (Winter 1995).

114

spoiled the joke. But its effect was not only to refashion Bourgeois's artistic persona through the substitution of a more enigmatic smile. When the museum cropped *Fillette* out of the picture, stripping the image of its erotic humor, it also enacted its own fetishistic scenario, presenting the head shot as a substitute. As Bourgeois herself has put it, "The glint in the eye refers to the thing I'm carrying. But they cut it. They cut it because the museum was so prudish."[52] The museum loves coldly, like a fetishist, but art has the potential to be humorous.

[52] Carolyn Treat, "Louise Bourgeois: Art Is a Guarantee for Sanity," interview, *Kunst & Museum Journal*, vol. 2, no. 6 (1991), 57.

FETISHES AND GHOSTS: MARX AND DERRIDA

Egidius Berns[1]

Paul Ricoeur's characterization of Marx, Nietzsche and Freud as the "three masters of suspicion" is widely known.[2] All three of these authors adhere to the notion that the ideas people have of various things, and above all of themselves, are not necessarily in agreement with these things and with this self. Marx's place in the line of the masters of suspicion is wholly inspired by what since Engels has been called his historical materialism. This is based on the distinction between, on the one hand, the "material transformation of the economic conditions of production"—the so-called infrastructure—and on the other, the "legal, political, religious, artistic or philosophic—in short, ideological forms in which men become conscious of this conflict and fight it out"—the so-called superstructure—and suggests that "it is not the consciousness of men that determines their existence, but rather their social existence that determines their consciousness."[3] In his well known section from *Das Kapital*,[4] "The Fetishism of Commodities and the Secret Thereof," Marx develops a more thorough and comprehensively thought-out analysis of the structural misconception of what is taking place. In this text Marx attempts to unravel the nature of what we, at first sight, experience as an everyday and quite simple thing: the economical good or, in his terms, "the commodity." In fact, the commodity keeps its true nature hidden from us and *therefore* enters into social developments taking place "behind [our] backs" (K 59/54). The theme that is brought to light with fetishism thus concerns the manner in which people become conscious of something. It concerns the manner in which ideas are formed and insights are gained. It is thus not a matter of a purely subjective process where social reality can appear in a different way to every individual. Rather, fetishism in Marx has much more to do with a theory that can explain why the manner that things *appear* is constitutive for reality.

[1] I would like to thank Rudi Visker and two anonymous referees from the *Tijdschrift voor Filosofie* for their critical commentary regarding an earlier version of this article.

[2] Paul Ricoeur, *De l'interprétation. Essai sur Freud*, (Paris : Seuil, 1965), 43.

[3] Karl Marx, *Zur Kritik der Politischen Ökonomie, Vorwort, MEW 13*. English translation: *A Contribution to the Critique of Political Economy*, trans. S.W. Ryazanskaya, ed. Maurice Dobb (New York: International Publishers, 1970), 21.

[4] K. Marx, *Das Kapital. Kritik der politischen Ökonomie. Erster Band* (Berlin: Dietz, 1969), *MEW 23*. References to this text will be noted by K, followed by the original page number of the German edition and the page number of the English translation. English translation: *Capital: A Critique of Political Economy, Vol. I*, trans. Samuel Moore and Edward Aveling, ed. Frederick Engels (London: Lawrence and Wishart, 1996).

In the case of fetishism, they appear in such a way that one's consciousness of them, in Ricoeur's terminology, is called "false," and that which is taken as true is often called "ideology."[5]

Marxism quickly lost ground in the eighties and nineties of the previous century, primarily due to the collapse of the Soviet regime. Instead of being perceived as a theory of suspicion, it mainly came to be seen as dogmatism. It was therefore remarkable that Jacques Derrida, who nevertheless continues to be a representative of suspicion in contemporary philosophy, brought out a book about Marx in 1993, entitled *Spectres de Marx*.[6] This book addresses the frequent appearance of the motive of the ghost in Marx's works. The *incipit* of *The Communist Manifesto*: "A specter is haunting Europe—the specter of communism," is a very well known example of this. It again shows Derrida's position with respect to Marx: the term 'ghost' is not only often found in Marx's work, but his diagnosis of modern, industrialized Europe is only possible thanks to an experience of the ghostly (SM 23/5). Since Marx's time, communism has been relegated to the status of a ghost, that is to say, a presence that has at the same time the ineffectiveness and insubstantiality of a "similacrum" (SM 31/10). "Ghost" thus means here a "furtive and ungraspable visibility of the invisible" (SM 27/7). For Marx, the world in his day was haunted by forces. In one of his later texts he still called the capitalist means of production "an enchanted, perverted, topsy-turvy world, in which Monsieur le Capital and Madame la Terre do their ghost-walking as social characters and at the same time directly as mere things."[7] Marx does not like phantoms any more than his adversaries do (SM 83/46). In his eyes, it is precisely the unreal character of social determinants that bring about the perniciousness of capitalism. Certainly, he sees this perniciousness as a result of a conspiracy of ghosts, yet his effort is precisely to free society from its enchantment with illusory forces in the service of truthful social processes. In this sense he wants to exorcise the phantom.

Fetishism in *Capital* is one of the figures of this ghost motif, and is above all the figure that expressly receives theoretical treatment by Marx. Derrida, in

---

5   Marx's analysis of fetishism is a continuation of his use of the term "ideology" which he frequently employed until 1852, but after that it no longer appears in his texts. According to Balibar, fetishism must offer a solution to the theoretical impasse that the notion of ideology had led Marx. *Cf.* E. Balibar, *La philosophie de Marx* (Paris: Éd. La Decouverte, 1993), 42 *ff*.

6   Jacques Derrida, *Spectres de Marx* (Paris: Galilée, 1993). References to this text will be noted by SM, followed by the original page number in the French edition and the page number in the English translation. English translation: *Specters of Marx*, trans. Peggy Kamuf (New York: Routledge, 1994).

7   K. Marx, *Das Kapital. Kritik der politischen Ökonomie, Dritter Band* (Berlin: Dietz, 1971) (*MEW 25*), 838. English translation, *Capital: A Critique of Political Economy, Vol. III, The Process of Capitalist Production as a Whole*, ed. Frederick Engels (London: Lawrence & Wishart, 1974), 830.

an earlier text, *Glas* (1974),[8] had already made an extensive detour into Marx's theory of fetishism. Both in *Spectres* and in *Glas* he shows great admiration for Marx's theory of fetishism. This evidently fits with his suspicion of the philosophical tradition.[9] At the same time, however, he also conducts an extensive criticism. This criticism attacks Marx's assumption that his own theory will avoid all fetishization and will have exorcised all enchantment by fetishes. The absolutizing of his own position is indeed what most hinders the modern reader of Marx and feeds the accusation of dogmatism that took root in the eighties and nineties. The opposition currently invoking this accusation goes so far as to forget Marx's text entirely, thus putting his fruitful insights at risk of being lost. Of course, such a stance concerning an author (who not twenty years ago was still counted among the great ones) has more to say about contemporary philosophy than about Marx. In this regard, the otherwise so somber Kant was incorrect when he, in the "secret article" concluding *Zum ewigen Frieden*, thought he could say that "the class of philosophers by virtue of its nature stands above suspicion of echoing propaganda."[10] Perhaps, however, contemporary problems with globalization will breathe new life into the attention given to Marx. It may then even be fortuitous that Marx is considered a "normal" thinker—albeit on an exceptional level. Derrida's reading of Marx's theory of fetishism in terms of ghosts can be helpful here. In this essay I will also pause to consider the relation between Marx's notion of fetish and fetishism and that of Derrida with respect to ghost and "hauntology," as he also calls his theory regarding ghosts.

In *Marx & Sons*,[11] on a number of occasions and in continuation of *Spectres de Marx*, Derrida suggests that the ghostly "is necessary to take account of the processes and consequences of ... metaphysicalization, abstraction, idealization, ideologization and fetishization" (M&S 61). It therefore concerns the manner in which people arrive at insights. Elsewhere he states that this haunting undoubtedly has something in common with ideology and fetishism but is not to be reduced to them (M&S 75). Derrida intends to question this irreducibility of the ghost to the fetish, and he does so because it puts him in a position to expose the link between fetishism and ontology. According to Derrida, a comparison of fetishes and ghosts makes it possible to

---

[8] J. Derrida, *Glas* (Paris: Galiée, 1974). Reference to this text indicated by GL followed by the original page number in the French edition and the page number in the English translation. English translation, *Glas*, trans. John P. Leavey Jr. and Richard Rand (Lincoln: University of Nebraska Press, 1986).

[9] "Deconstruction would have been impossible and unthinkable in a pre-Marxist space," SM 151/92.

[10] Immanuel Kant, *Zum ewigen Frieden*, *Werkausgabe Band XI* (Frankfurt am Main: Suhrkamp, 1977), 228.

[11] J. Derrida, (Paris: PUF/Galilée, 2002). References to this text are indicated by M&S followed by the page number.

call philosophy as ontology into question. Particularly in Marx, as a discourse about the presence of being, this comparison views his political philosophy as an ontology (M&S 12,13,16) in the form of a historical teleology. The processes of fetishization that Marx describes in *Capital* will remain loyal to the foremost ontological presupposition, namely, the possibility of presence which, in principle, allows for an absolute position in which fetishism is exorcised. This loyalty, however, cannot be debated from the outside, as this in turn would suppose a firm ground on which fetishistic enchantment would be neutralized. One of the characteristics of deconstruction is in fact that the critique occurs from the inside. In the texts where Marx argues for the exorcism of fetishism, it must also be shown how a type of fetishization is still active, annulling the possibility of a complete absolution. This generalization of fetishism at the cost of its exorcism indicates precisely the point where the fetish turns out to be a ghost and where hauntology escapes ontology.

We will focus on three questions in what follows. First, in what sense is a fetish a ghost? This is the theme of *Spectres de Marx* (in particular from page 231 to 252/125 to 158). Second, how does an ontological presupposition characterize the fetish? *Spectres de Marx* treats of this as well (specifically pages 253*ff.*/159*ff.*), as does *Glas* (primarily pages 230-4/207-211). Third, in what sense is this not the case for the ghost? In order to make the comparison between Marx's fetish and Derrida's ghost, in the opening section we will explain what Marx says about fetishism. In the two sections that follow, we will show in what sense a fetish is a ghost, and then we will address the ontological kernel of fetishism. We will close with a few considerations regarding the ghost dialectic with which hauntology distinguishes itself from ontology.

1. Fetish and Commodity

"Has this thing appeared again tonight?"
Hamlet I, 1

The famous fourth section of Chapter I in *Capital* talks about trivial and at first glance obvious things such as merchandise and money in terms of "secret," "riddle," "mystery," "theological niceties," "dancing tables," "phantasmagorical form," a "sensuous supersensuous thing,"—*ein sinnlich übersinnliches Ding*—of "magic and necromancy"—*Zauber und Spuk*—and, of course, "fetishes." For Marx, a commodity is indeed a fetish in the sense that "in it the social character of men's labour appears to them—*zurück-spiegelt*—as an objective character stamped upon the product of that labour" (K 86/82-3). Social relations thus assume the form of the concrete and perceptible character of commodities, thereby hiding their social origin from view. In Marx's view, people move around in a word of visible things believing that what they see actually possess the qualities that in fact arise from social processes, more specifically those of production and thus, in Marx's eyes, of exploitation and class struggle. Therefore, that which is attributed to the naturalness of things in fact arises from their social essence. "There it is a definite social relation between men, that assumes, in their eyes, the fantastic form of a relation between things" (ibid.).

In order to explain how the social character of commodities appear in people's minds to be the natural qualities of concrete things, Marx returns to his explanation of the commodity preceding the explanation in the fetish section, and for which the fetish section serves as a conclusion. The commodity, as it is called there, is in the first place a concrete thing that, according to its properties, satisfies human wants of one sort or another, and is therefore useful. In this regard the commodity represents a use value (K 49/46). Marx calls this use value the "substance of all wealth" and the "material depository" (K 50/46) of that which the commodity will seem to be. Thanks to its use value, commodities are thus visible and useful for the consumer.

But the economic good Marx calls "commodity," characteristic of the capitalist mode of production, is more than just a use value. It always also presents itself as the quantitative (but constantly changing) relation in which one use value is exchanged for another (K 50/46). Marx calls this, in agreement with the tradition since Aristotle, the exchange value of the commodity. To say that the capitalist mode of production produces commodities means that the (otherwise unavoidable) production of use values occurs with a view toward the production of goods that can be exchanged on the market—thus with a view toward their exchange value. In Marx's opinion, capitalism is therefore a further development of what Aristotle called the chrematistic that, with the production of use values, equally sought "where and how the greatest profits might be made out of [exchange]."[12]

According to Marx, the possibility of exchanging one commodity for another points to the fact that they have something in common. This commonality cannot, in his view, be ascribed to their use value, for here they differ in quality. From this Marx draws a conclusion that, for *Capital* in general and fetishism in particular, may be of decisive importance: "The two things must therefore be equal to a third, which in itself is neither the one nor the other" (K 51/47). This 'third thing' that can explain the exchange value of goods is, in Marx's view, *distinct* from the use value of the goods concerned, and thus also from that which provides these goods with their visibility and materiality and makes them useful with respect to the satisfaction of consumer needs. It therefore remains invisible, becomes an abstraction and escapes one's awareness as a consumer.

---

[12] Aristotle, *The Politics*, trans. T.A. Sinclair (1962), revised by J. Saunders (New York: Penguin Books, 1981), 1257 b5.

This third thing, which all commodities have in common, resides in the condition that they are always products of labor. 'Labor' here does not really refer to the various concrete forms of labor (the clothier, the baker, etc.), for these forms constitute precisely the differences between commodities. Rather, labor must here refer to what makes the commodities equal and thus turns them into "congelations" or "crystals" of the same social entity that Marx calls "abstract labor." In Marx's view, the exchange value of commodities is therefore determined by the amount of abstract labor required to bring them into existence.

Capital concerns this third thing, the social process whereby concrete forms of labor (on the labor market) are transformed into the abstract, and this under the capitalistic condition of private ownership of the means of production which is always accompanied by class conflict and exploitation. Thanks to private ownership, a few—the capitalists—have the means of production at their disposal, while the others—the workers—are denied access. The latter are left with nothing to provide for their subsistence but their labor power, which they must offer as a commodity on the labor market. There they face the same fate as all other commodities, namely, to be paid in accordance with their exchange value; i.e., as a congelation of abstract labor. Otherwise stated; they are paid with the expenses required to create and maintain a labor force. The capitalist thereby acquires a productive force that, when joined with capital goods, creates more exchange value than it costs. The difference is the surplus value with which the capitalist exploits the worker, provided the former has the capital goods at his or her disposal and the latter remains deprived of them.

The consumer does not actually enter into exchange because he or she is interested in what the commodities have in common, but rather because of their differences. For the consumer is after a means to satisfy a need, a means that is not possessed, but which can be acquired in exchange for a means at his or her disposal. And thus the fact that commodities have a certain value with respect to one another is not accounted for by reference to the third thing and the social processes at their basis, but rather in relation to the visible and material characteristics of commodities. In a social system that, like capitalism, is based on the production of commodities, social relations take the form of relations between things.

This "fetishism" finds its ultimate form in money (K 90/86, see also K 97/93). In opposition to what has been suggested above, exchange in our society does not take place between two commodities, but through the mediation of money. Thanks to money, the value of commodities can be expressed as a price. In Marx's view, money possesses this potential because it is a commodity and thus has an exchange value with respect to all other commodities—their price—which finally, and invisibly, is determined by the expenditure of abstract labor in the generation of money. That the one commodity has a higher price than the other is due to the fact that the more expensive commodity contains more abstract labor than the cheaper one, in terms of the abstract labor contained in a unit of money. But money is also a use value that people like to have in their wallets. They then think they are "rich", even if this merely concerns pieces of paper and metal.

These two aspects of money—exchange and use value—converge,[13] yet are completely unrelated with respect to their origin. People like to have money *because* it is exchangeable with *all* commodities. That all commodities may in this manner be brought under the universal denominator of money indicates, according to Marx, that all commodities have something in common. This takes shape in the social process—ever so painful, in his view, because it goes together with exploitation—of transforming concrete labor into the abstract on the labor market. This social process, however, completely takes the form of the price-relation between things. The social character of money—what we would now speak of as monetary trust—is reflected in people's minds as price relations. Money thus expresses its social nature as the price of things, and precisely so its social nature is obscured, torn apart by exploitation and class conflict. This is brought most clearly to the fore in the wage that, as the price established for labor-power by the mechanism of the labor market, veils the exploitation of the laborer.

Money is thus, in a double sense, the completion of fetishism. In the first, dialectical sense, money brings fetishism to its *end* and thereby opens the path to its elimination. Thanks to money, the communality, which remained hidden behind the price relation between things, appears quite emphatically in the foreground as something exceeding the materiality of differences between commodities in favor of their coherence, and therefore sets people in search of something that, until then, remained invisible: the social origin of value. Money, more than the exchange value of normal goods, brings a certain abstraction or ideality into economic life. Money can nevertheless only bring about this change because, secondly, it is also *the paradigm* of a fetish, for nowhere else is such a deficiency so coherently established in the division of society and the meaning of trust than in the neutralization and homogenization of all tensions brought about by the price formation of the market system. Whether this second meaning, which is incompatible with the first, gives money its aporetic character or not is the problem Derrida addresses.

---

[13] "If commodities seem *to have* an exchange value, money, in its turn, seems *to be* exchange value itself." E. Balibar, *op. cit.*, 58-9.

2. Fetish as Ghost

"The body is with the King, but the King is not with the body."
Hamlet, IV, 3.

The interpretive framework used by Marx in connection with fetishism is evidently that of religion, though he also has an economic explanation in mind. "In order, therefore, to find an analogy," as he emphasizes, "we must have recourse to the mist-enveloped regions of the religious world. In that world the productions of the human brain appear as independent beings endowed with life, and entering into relation both with one another and the human race" (K 86/83). We have the habit of imagining the economy as a totality of natural, if not material, things and processes. The economy would be the best representative of the world in its so-called materiality and naturalness. The economist can, despite all historical and anthropological studies to the contrary, hardly imagine a society without market activities; in his eyes they form the natural aspect of every society. In everyday language, the word "materialism" stands for being enmeshed in this economic world, whereas in the past it was the object of economic science as often defined by the so-called "material definition," namely, the production and consumption of material goods. Marx, on the contrary, accords these apparently obvious materialities the status of phantoms, analogous to religious objects. In their physical materiality they seem to be purely what they are, to be their own origin, but in fact they lead a shadowy existence. In relation to this existence, Marx means that the economic world is not comprised solely of evident things and natural processes, but always contains a dimension of consciousness as well. It is by means of this consciousness that the world is also defined by ideas, interpretations, insights, in short, abstractions, even if they are—as he has shown with commodity fetishism—false. Above all, these aspects of consciousness are not subjective. They are, rather, constitutive of how reality appears. The world is thereby no longer made up of stable things, but of thin air, of phantoms riddled with abstraction.

One could say that the world is also shadowy for Derrida. Access to an original presentation of things is denied us. Even more, things only seem to enjoy a presentation that can lay claim to originality *because* we are denied access to it. The affirmation of their presence is inextricably linked with the belief in it. This is why Marx's religious frame of interpretation with respect to fetishism does not surprise him.

Derrida already thematized this problematic in his first works with the term "original supplement,"[14] which means both supplement of the origin and original supplement. What appears original to our consciousness is thus an

---

[14]   *"supplément d'origine." Cf.* J. Derrida, *La voix et le phénomène* (Paris : PUF, 1967), 97-9 ; *De la grammatologie* (Paris : Minuit, 1967), 225-6.

addition to the origin, and not the origin itself, which is made possible only by means of that addition. This addition is not in principle superfluous, but is precisely something without which that which it manifests could not be what it is, and which therefore only "is" in connection with what it is not and what is added to it. Such a supplement is an irreducible substitute and thus an external supplement for something that, from inside out, lacks presence. Thus the exchange value in the commodity haunts every use value. Use values, these obvious things seeming to surround us on all sides, only exist insofar as they are haunted by the phantom of their exchange value, expressed as prices with the assistance of money, and through which they also always belong to a social system.

What Derrida calls "ghost" is a new figure of the supplement insofar that it is also[15] active in the experience of the ghostly that enabled Marx to formulate his diagnosis of modern Europe and thoroughly examine it in his analysis of the commodity as fetish. The analogy with the nether world of religion is important for this. Derrida considers three of the characteristics that Marx ascribes to the commodity as fetish as also applying to ghosts. That which Derrida wishes to indicate with the notion of ghost or phantom can therefore be clarified in view of Marx's analysis of the fetish-character of the commodity. The three characteristics we are concerned with point to three specific features of his deconstructive philosophy—the transgression of phenomenology; the connection between life and death, freedom and mechanism, naturalness and artificiality; and finally, mirroring repetition, which is also always a displacement. One often finds these features reappearing in other contexts in Derrida's works.

First, the commodity as fetish is ghostly in the sense that it is "a sensuous supersensuous thing"[16] (K, 86/83). The analogon of the fetish thereby remains the religious, but this is, in Derrida's view, no longer of a "spiritual" nature, as long as we understand this word in the traditional sense. It indeed relates to the extrasensory and invisible, but this occurs, in opposition to the spiritual, in a sensual manner. At issue is still merely one thing, namely, a commodity or a piece of currency. At first sight, it seems obvious that the meaning of a commodity begins and ends with its capacity to satisfy needs as a use value.

---

[15] Also, and thus not exclusively, for Derrida also uses the term in connection with other authors. The verb 'hanter,' 'haunt' but also 'associate with,' 'well-attended' and 'wander around in,' has even become one of his favorite expressions to set straight the relation of the *supplément d'origine*.

[16] [ed. note:] The original text reads "Quidproquo werden die Arbeitsprodukte Waren, sinnlich übersinnliche oder gesellschaftliche Dinge." I have translated as "sensuous supersensuous" to retain the paradoxical sense of the original German. The English translation reads: "This is the reason why the products of labour become commodities, social things whose qualities are at the same time perceptible and imperceptible by the senses." A page earlier, "ein sinnlich übersinnliches Ding" is even more flatly translated as "something transcendent" (K 85/82).

This obviousness, however, only serves to hide its deeper meaning, namely, to be a product of social labor. To this Derrida links the conclusion that the relation of the commodity to its phenomenality becomes problematic (SM 241-2/152). The significance of commodities is, after all, not what these goods, in their quantity of use values, present themselves to be. This significance is also not purely ideal or spiritual, but rather "sensuous supersensuous." The commodity as fetish is therefore a phantom because it concerns a thing without a phenomenon, taking refuge in the body of a use value which is not its body.

Then, the commodity as fetish is as ghostly as the religious because it, in its inertia, appears "as [an] independent being endowed with life" (K 86/83), and seems capable of development by generating its own movement—moving about freely (K 85/82). Simultaneously a dead artifact and yet capable of animated development; thus not living but surviving, the commodity possesses a sort of mechanical freedom, a technical life that can expand infinitely.

Finally, the commodity as fetish is a ghost because it is not reflected in the mirror. What is typical of a ghost is that it can see me without being seen. It thus interrupts the reflexivity of vision. The commodity is social in the sense that it, in an endlessly expanding process, not only links more and more commodities to one another but also brings together more and more people. The mystery that Marx wants to clarify concerns how the growing social relations among people are transformed into relations between commodities, money included, as soon as these commodities enter the market to be exchanged. How, that is, human interaction is changed into object relations despite the fact that these object relations originate in human, social relations. The solution to this riddle is that commodities, which also applies to ghosts, can interrupt mutual reflection and thus need not offer themselves as a reflection in people's minds of what they are, namely, their social being, but can assume the shape of their own bodies as use values. Social relations are thereby naturalized. Owing to the ghostly character of commodities:

> The relation of the producers to the sum total of their own labour is presented to them as a social relation, existing not between themselves, but between the products of their labour. This is the reason why the products of labour become commodities, social things whose qualities are at the same time perceptible and imperceptible by the senses (K 86/83).

3. Fetishism and Ontology

> "Horatio says 'tis but our fantasy, and will not let belief take hold of him."
> Hamlet I, 1

In the previous section I described how a fetish can become phantomagical. This is not intended to mean, however, that a ghost can be reduced to a fetish. Rather, it is an attempt to reformulate fetishism as a type of hauntology. In an early phase of his work, namely in the 1974 work *Glas*, Derrida demonstrated the ontological presupposition of fetishism. According to Derrida, fetishism always assumes a philosophy of the presence of the thing itself. In Ricoeur's terminology, one could say that it is a theory of false consciousness based on the presumption that true consciousness is possible. The kernel of this is the decidable distinction between the use value and the exchange value of a commodity as assumed by Marx. For Marx, it seems indisputable that the fetish only appears on the stage with exchange value, and thus leaves use value behind the curtain, undisturbed. It is precisely for this reason that the natural and objective qualities of use value, which would fit with the supposed human self and its needs, can completely erase the social origin of the exchange value of commodities and can become a fetish of it. The consequence of this is that the processes of fetishization for Marx remain limited to the mode of production that is marked by exchange value, namely capitalism, and that use value can offer an ontological support for modes of production that both preceded the production of commodities, such as primitive communism, as well as what will come after, such as communism, where the processes of fetishization have been exorcised.

This structure of fetishism determines the most important theories of *Capital*, such as the following: 1) The previously sketched value-theory and its starting point in the possibility of a strict distinction between use value and exchange value: 2) The theory of capital as a social relation where profit is explained by the exploitation of one class by another, concealed under the system of wages: 3) The theory of the transformation of values into market prices, which shows why values remain invisible and why bourgeois economists allow themselves to be fooled by market prices: 4) The theory of the final determination of a superstructure as the visible location of class struggle by an infrastructure whose influences remain invisible.[17] Above all, one may claim that *Capital* tries to exorcise fetishism. This book allows one to see how fetishism can be understood through the commodity form, a form that can be identified as the distinguishing trait of the capitalist mode of

---

[17] For further development of this general structure of *Capital* I refer to chapter 5 of my *Kringloop en Woekering. Een deconstructieve filosofie van de economie* (Amsterdam: Boom, 1998).

production. It also aims to prove how capitalism digs its own grave, thereby actually removing the conditions of possibility for fetishism.

In order to sell one's products and convert them into surplus value, the capitalist, as it so happens, must enter into competition with other capitalists. This drives one to position oneself as strongly as possible with respect to the competition. That is only possible with the help of technological developments and thus investment in capital goods. The share of capital goods at the cost of labor's share thereby increases. This causes redundancies in the labor force. But it occurs at the expense of the source of profit, the surplus value, since this is only attained through the exploitation of labor. Caught between increasing unemployment and pauperization (*Verelendung*) on the one hand, and an increasing concentration of the means of production in fewer and fewer hands in order to escape the drying up of profits on the other, capitalism finds itself in crisis. This is determined by the antithesis, on the one hand, between the social character of production, as appears in the increasing concentration of the means of production and the consequences this has for employment, and on the other, the private character of access to the means of production. With this historical development of capitalism, *the thing itself*, namely, the social origin of the products of labor is stripped of its phantasmagorical *substitutes* and as such enters into presence. Instead of continuing to endure the process of production as an external process of things "[somewhat like] the law of gravity [that] asserts itself when a house falls about our ears" (K 89/86), the workers, "carrying on their work with the means of production in common," will experience this work in such a way that "the labour power of all the different individuals is *consciously* applied as the combined labour power of the community" (K 92/89, emphasis added). Marx therefore not only reveals, in a masterly fashion, the origin of these substitutes in the capitalist mode of production, but also the inevitability of their actual disappearance. But to do so, he must limit the possibility of fetishism to the production of commodities specific to capitalism. In one and the same gesture, communism is acquitted of this charge and the door to dogmatism is thrown open.

The logic we have seen at work here in Marx's analysis regarding fetishism has a general structure. It determines the relation between the thing itself and its substitute in such a way that this substitute, behind which the thing itself lies hidden, ultimately disappears in favor of the thing itself. Both terms of the relation can be distinguished in a decidable manner, for the substitute refers to a thing that, in its turn, cannot be a substitute, and thus *as such* must be able to exist and enter into presence. This general structure therefore explains not only why, at a given moment, there is a "false" consciousness which remains enchanted with the substitutes, but also the inevitability of the insight into the thing itself. Or, in the words of Ricoeur concerning Marx, what this master of suspicion wants "is the liberation of *praxis* through the knowledge of necessity; but this liberation is not to be separated from a 'becoming conscious' that triumphantly refers back to the mystifications of false consciousness."[18] In the end, after the revolution, it is assumed that the social essence of production—which until then had remained hidden as a result of the obviousness and naturalness of commodities; the wage structure as the transformation of concrete labor into an abstraction and the conflicts in the superstructure—will become present and, owing to this visibility, will make possible a self-conscious expenditure of social labor by the individual forces of labor. Likewise, Marx assumes that the origin of society is found in use value rather than exchange value, the latter being the sole cause of fetishistic effects (SM 253, *ff./*159*ff.*). Consequently, these effects have no influence on use values, which can then serve as the basis for a post-revolutionary economy in which fetishism will be exorcised.

I have already referred to the importance of religion for the interpretation of fetishism. In this connection, one again discerns the general structure of the fetish. It determines the attitude not only of critics of religion such as Marx (GL 230-1/206), but also of religious zealots. Both fight for the thing itself and against substitutes. For the zealots, the thing itself is of course the *Jenseits*, while for the critics it is the *Diesseits*. But both share the desire to be free from animated substitutes which block the vision of the thing itself and threaten to poison its essence, thereby endangering the ability to distinguish the thing itself from the substitute. Faith in this ability, thanks to which fetishism can be exorcised, is precisely what Derrida in this instance calls ontology. "*Ontology is a conjuration*" (SM 255/161). Also in *Glas* he states that the fetish:

> is a substitute—for the thing itself... . According to this minimal conceptual determination, the fetish is opposed to the presence of the thing itself, to truth, signified truth for which the fetish is a substitutive signifier... . Something—the thing—is no longer itself a substitute... . If there were no thing, the concept fetish would lose its invariant kernel... . If what has always been called fetish, in all the critical discourses, implies the reference to a nonsubstitutive thing, there should be somewhere—and that is the truth of the fetish, the relation of the fetish to truth— ... a decidable opposition of the fetish to the nonfetish ... of *Ersatz* to non*Ersatz* (GL 234/210).

---

[18] P. Ricoeur, *op. cit.*, 43.

4. Dialectic of Ghosts

> "There are more things in heaven and earth, Horatio, than are dreamt of in your philosophy... . The time is out of joint."
> Hamlet, I, 5

The previous paragraph has perhaps, and not unjustifiably, left the reader with the image of an external critique of fetishism. This could make one wonder how Derrida's critique of fetishism can itself escape the antithesis between the substitute and the thing itself. It is on this point that the phantomization of fetishism must offer solace, and where in his eyes ontology transmutates into hauntology. The latter is based on a deconstructive reading of fetishism, a reading no longer developed from the outside, but from the inside out. This reading can no longer "prove" that the thing itself does not exist, for then it would begin to function as the thing itself; such a reading can only demonstrate that the thing itself, in every factual formulation that intends to determine it, is delayed. The reformulation of fetishism in terms of ghosts is then found in Marx's text only by pointing to the activity of fetishism at the moment that it should have been exorcised.

Marx's treatment of accumulation offers a prime example of the possibility of a similar deconstruction. To analyze accumulation, Marx once again calls upon religious motives, namely the Fall. Capitalist accumulation assumes the presence of workers who rely solely on their labor power for their means of subsistence. Their presence can in fact explain surplus value and thus capitalistic accumulation, but cannot itself be explained by these factors. "The whole movement, therefore, seems to turn in a vicious circle, out of which we can only get by supposing a primitive accumulation preceding capitalistic accumulation; an accumulation not the result of the capitalist mode of production, but its starting point" (K 741/704). This original accumulation is not, according to Marx, the result of "[on the one hand] diligent, intelligent, and, above all frugal elite; [and on the other hand] lazy rascals ..." (ibid.), as is often claimed, but rather of a violent divorce of the producer from the means of production. "The dull compulsion of economic relations completes the subjection of the labourer to the capitalist," but is itself the fruit of "direct force, outside economic conditions," the "power of the state" which "the bourgeoisie ... wants and uses" (K 765/726). In the case of original accumulation, Marx does not hesitate to call on a substitute, namely political and thus superstructural violence, in order to explain the thing itself, namely, the social conditions of production. In the course of Marx's theoretical research the fetish develops from something that the thing itself substitutes, to something that has always already included this thing. Hereby both distinctions become irresolvable. In the course of its development, the thing itself increasingly withdraws and seems every time again to be taken up in the fetish that is supposed to replace it. Substitution, or if one likes, fetishization, is therefore more original than the distinction that it establishes.

In fact, Derrida's doubt regarding the possibility of a strict differentiation between use and exchange value rests on a similar generalization of fetishism. In this connection, it must above all be emphasized that the deconstruction of ontology by means of a generalization of fetishism is not a dogmatic affair, but goes together with a consistent view concerning the manner in which people are conscious of the world. We have, on a number of occasions, indicated that fetishism is also involved in the manner insights are formed. This is the case if we recognize the same form in different versions of this form. That means that in understanding the world, a process of abstraction from the concrete conditions of existence is set in motion, and this leads to an ideality whose different versions are but repetitions. It always leads, to be sure, to a *supersensuous*, but it remains *sensuous* and, for this reason, ghostly. Every version can, in effect, only be a transforming repetition—Derrida calls this iteration—of ideality, and this ideality is always affected by the transformation that sets the nomination in motion, such that what one becomes conscious of "changes into a sensuous supersensuous thing." This ghost-schema is always active as soon as something happens to us and we try to incorporate it. Derrida then also emphasizes the inconsistency of Marx's rejection of the possibility of use value becoming fetishized. Marx differentiates use value from exchange value on analytically solid grounds and according to the tradition of economic theory.[19] This does not, however, mean that he can exclude use value from fetishization, for recognition of the form of the use value assumes that use value originates and depends, "however minimal it may have been, on an idealization that permits one to identify it as the same throughout possible repetitions" (SM 254/160). Without the ghostly movement of fetishization, "one could not even form the concept ... of use value" (SM 256/161).

Derrida's phantomizing of fetishism thus generalizes it, so that even the construction of ideality and comprehensibility, along with the concept of fetishism itself, are included in the overall picture. But, to remain consistent, Derrida must contest the possibility of exorcising fetishism and limiting it to a particular historical period. Use values are also fetishizable. This means that use values are already manipulated from inside out by the fetishizing effects that Marx accords to exchange value. Calculation and the chrematistic are not to be kept out of the *oikos*, of what is proper(ty) and what is one's own.[20]

---

[19] There are also solid grounds for the major theories in *Capital*. In the third section I have already shown that the structure of fetishism seems to be decisive for these theories. Doubt with respect to the possibility of this structure will have repercussions for these theories as well. But that does not yet mean that they, *for this reason*, would lose their significance. Their truth claims are changed, but not the importance that their content may represent.

[20] "As soon as there is a monetary sign—and first of all sign—that is, differance and credit, the *oikos* is opened and cannot dominate its limit. On the threshold of

From this one must not conclude that this generalization of fetishism "entail[s] a general phantasmagorization in which everything would indifferently become commodity, in an equivalence of prices" (SM 258/162-3). This conclusion of indifference could become involved, for without the key—without the thing itself—the one fetish can only be exchanged for another. The fetish is once again unmasked. But this unmasking immediately creates a new fetish. Derrida is regularly accused of this sort of "nihilism" and "relativism". The substitution is indeed more original than the difference between the terms that it establishes, and can therefore no longer be exorcised. But this still does not eliminate the fact that the difference cannot be avoided. Substitution thus calls on a dialectic of opposition between the substitute and the thing itself, but owing to the undecidability of the opposition, one must at the same time be aware of the impossibility of a solution for this opposition. More positively stated: every solution proposed by the dialectic can only be a compromise. "Between the logic of the undecidable and the compromise," Derrida says, "there is an irreducible link, so long as there is life. The idea of compromise implies an attempt to control the opposition which in fact offers no space for a solution, for a sentence. It is the undecidability that sets all things in motion, the fetishization, the compromise, but I do not think that the undecidable can be understood in another way than by compromise."[21] This imitation of dialectic, this ghost dialectic, is far from meaningless. It spurs one on to knowledge. It pushes one to "a more refined and more rigorous reformulation" (SM 258/163) of the terms of the distinction "and transforms [them] into a co-implication" (SM 256/161).

This plea for rationality is really but one side of the question. There is still another reason why the generalization of fetishism does not lead to indifference. This has to do with what one could call a sort of Levinassian twist. There where the thing itself traditionally establishes a ground for morality, its loss indeed offers new opportunities for morality. The generalization of fetishism implies, in effect, a relation of consciousness to an exteriority that consciousness cannot make its own. Derrida speaks in this context primarily of the singular and the other. Consciousness is marked by this aporetic relation. It is a relation with the other and can therefore not avoid

itself, the family no longer knows its bounds. This is at the same time its originary ruin and the chance for any kind of hospitality. It is, like counterfeit money, the chance of the gift itself." J. Derrida, *Donner le temps* (Paris: Galilée, 1991), 200. English translation, *Given Time: 1. Counterfeit Money*, trans. Peggy Kamuf (Chicago: University of Chicago Press, 1992), 158. Exchange value thus forever haunts use value. But the reverse is also true. If the difference between use and exchange value is no longer assured, the sphere of exchange value—the economy—is open to what is traditionally ascribed to use value and to what is seen as uneconomic, like a gift. Accordingly, what is called "economy" is a process that cannot avoid the violence of abstraction, but at the same time it leaves room for the incalculable.

[21] J. Derrida, *Les fins de l'homme* (Paris: Galilée, 1981), 114.

the dialectical movement described above. At the same time it is not actually capable of completing the dialectical movement and remains in wait of its appropriation by the other. This powerlessness—which otherwise is unidentifiable *as such*, but is rather indirectly manifested in an actual failure of the dialectic—indicates the limitation of the power of reason. The activity of consciousness is marked by a characteristically passive relation to the other. According to Derrida, this must be understood positively. This activity is not driven by nostalgia for the thing itself, but is an answer to "the other". The haunting of fetishism is not the result of an inability to reach the thing itself, but of a passive moment in rationality that points to a relation to an outside, which in its ever-anterior and irreducible exteriority once again incites affirmation.

BIBLIOGRAPHY

This bibliography details most of the works referenced in the essays comprising this volume. Works by Freud cited as *SE* are from the *Standard Edition of the Complete Works of Sigmund Freud*, 24 vols. (London: Hogarth Press, 1966-74).

Primary Sources

Freud, Sigmund. "'Civilized' Sexual Morality and Modern Nervous Illness." In *SE IX*, 177- 203.
—. "Fetishism." In *SE XXI*, 152-7.
—. "Fräulein Elisabeth von R.." In Joseph Breuer and Sigmund Freud, *Studies on Hysteria*, trans. James and Alix Strachey, ed. James Strachey, Alix Strachey, and Angela Richards, 202-55. London: Penguin, 1974.
—. *Group Psychology and the Analysis of the Ego*. In *SE XVIII*, 65-143.
—. "Humor." In *SE XXI*, 159-66.
—. "The Infantile Genital Organization (An Interpretation into the Theory of Sexuality)." In *On Sexuality: Three Essays on the Theory of Sexuality and Other Works*, trans. James Strachey, ed. Angela Richards, 303-12. London: Penguin, 1991.
—. *Jokes and Their Relation to the Unconscious*. In *SE VIII*
—. *New Introductory Lectures on Psychoanalysis*. In *SE XXII*
—. "On the Genesis of Fetishism." In "Freud and Fetishism: Previously Unpublished Minutes of the Vienna Psychoanalytic Society," ed. and trans. Louis Rose, *Psychoanalytic Quarterly LVII* (1988): 147-66.
—. "On Narcissism: An Introduction." In *SE XIV*, 67-102.
—. "On the Universal Tendency to Debasement in the Sphere of Love." In *SE XI*, 177-90.
—. "Splitting of the Ego in the Process of Defence." In *SE XXIII*, 271-8.
—. *Three Essays on the Theory of Sexuality*, *SE VII*, 130-243.
—. "Two Encyclopaedia Articles." In *SE XVIII*, 233-59.

Lacan, Jacques. *The Ego in Freud's Theory and in the Technique of Psychoanalysis 1954- 1955: The Seminar of Jacques Lacan, Book II*, trans. Sylvana Tomaselli. Cambridge: Cambridge University Press, 1988.
—. *The Ethics of Psychoanalysis, 1959-1960: The Seminar of Jacques Lacan, Book VII*, ed. Jacques-Alain Miller, trans. Dennis Porter. London: Tavistock/Routledge, 1992.

—. *The Four Fundamental Concepts of Psychoanalysis*, trans. Alan Sheridan, ed. Jacques- Alain Miller. New York: Norton, 1981.

—. *Le Seminaire. Livre XXI. Les non-dupes errent/Les noms du père, 1973-74*, unpublished.

—. *Le Séminaire de Jacques Lacan: Livre VIII, Le transfert 1960-1961*. Paris: Éditions du Seuil, 1991.

Marx, Karl. *Capital: A Critique of Political Economy, Vol. I*, trans. Samuel Moore and Edward Aveling. In *Karl Marx, Fridrich Engels, Collected Works Vol. 35*. London: Lawrence and Wishart, 1996.

—. *Capital: A Critique of Political Economy, Vol. III, The Process of Capitalist Production as a Whole*, ed. Friedrich Engels. London: Lawrence and Wishart, 1974.

—. *A Contribution to the Critique of Political Economy*, trans. S.W. Ryazanskaya, ed. Maurice Dobb. New York: International Publishers, 1970.

—. "The Leading Article in No. 179 of the *Kölnische Zeitung*." In Karl Marx and Friedrich Engels, *Collected Works*, Vol. 1. 184-202. New York: International, 1975.

—. *Theories of Surplus Value*, part 3, trans. Jack Cohen and S. W. Ryazanskaya. Moscow: Progress, 1971.

—. *Theses on Feuerbach*, *IV* (version edited by Engels). In *Collected Works*, Vol. 5.

—. *Zur Kritik der Politischen Ökonomie, Vorwort*. In *Karl Marx, Friedrich Engels: Werke, Band 13*. Berlin: Dietz Verlag, 1975.

Marx, Karl and Friedrich Engels. *The German Ideology*, vol. 1, trans. Clemens Dutt. In *Collected Works*, Vol. 5: *Marx and Engels: 1845-47*. London: Lawrence and Wishart, 1976.

Secondary Sources

Abraham, Karl. "Manifestations of the Female Castration Complex."In *Karl Abraham: Selected Papers on Psychoanalysis*, trans. Douglas Bryan and Alix Strachey. London: Maresfield Library, 1927; reprint, 1988.

Alloway, Lawrence. "Art," *The Nation*, March 27, 1972

Aristotle. *The Politics*, trans. T.A. Sinclair (1962), revised by J. Saunders. New York: Penguin Books, 1981.

Balibar, Étienne. *La philosophie de Marx*. Paris: Éd. La Decouverte, 1993.

Baudrillard, Jean. "Fetishism and Ideology: The Semiological Reduction." In *For a Critique of the Political Economy of the Sign*, trans. Charles Levin. St. Louis: Telos Press, 1981.

Berns, Egidius. *Kringloop en Woekering. Een deconstructieve filosofie van de economie*. Amsterdam: Boom, 1998.

Binet, Alfred. *Le fétichisme dans l'amour*. Paris : Edition La bibliothèque des Introuvables, 2000.

Bloch, Susi. "An Interview with Louise Bourgeois," *Art Journal*, vol. 35, no. 4 (Summer 1976).

Bowlby, Rachel "Still Crazy after All These Years." In *Between Feminism and Psychoanalysis*, ed. Teresa Brennan. New York: Routledge, 1989.

Brenson, Michael Francis. "The Early Work of Giacometti, 1925-1935." Ph.D. diss., The Johns Hopkins University, 1974.

Brosses, Charles de. *Du culte des dieux fétiches, ou Parallèle de l'ancienne religion de l'Egypte avec la religion actuelle de Nigritie*. France: Fayard, Corpus des Oeuvres de Philosophie en Langue Française, 1988.

Cassirer, Ernst. *The Philosophy of Symbolic Forms: Vol.2, Mythical Thought*, trans. Ralph Manheim. New Haven: Yale University Press, 1955.

Comte, Auguste. *Oeuvres d'Auguste Comte* Vol. 5, *Cours de Philosophie Positive*, 5th edition. Paris: Au Siège de la Société Positiviste, 1894.

Dadoun, Roger. "Le Fétichisme dans le film d'horreur." In *Objets du fétichisme*, 227-48. Paris : Nouvelle Revue de Psychanalyse, Numéro 2 (automne, 1970).

Deleuze, Gilles. *Présentation de Sacher-Masoch*. Paris: Ed. de Minuit, Coll. 'Arguments 32, 1967.

Derrida, Jacques. *De la grammatologie*. Paris: Minuit, 1967.

—. *Les fins de l'homme*. Paris: Galilée, 1981.

—. *Given Time: 1. Counterfeit Money*, trans. Peggy Kamuf. Chicago: University of Chicago Press, 1992.

—. *Glas*, trans. John P. Leavey, Jr. and Richard Randl. Lincoln: University of Nebraska Press, 1986.

—. *Marx & Sons*. Paris: PUF/Galilée, 2002.

—. *Specters of Marx*, trans. Peggy Kamuf. New York: Routledge, 1994.

—. *La voix et le phénomène*. Paris : PUF, 1967.

Doane, Janice and Hodges, Devon. *From Klein to Kristeva: Psychoanalytic Feminism and the Search for the "Good Enough" Mother*. Ann Arbor: University of Michigan Press, 1992.

Eliot, George. *The Mill on the Floss*. London: Everyman, 1996.

Foster, Hal. *Compulsive Beauty*. Cambridge: MIT Press, 1993.

Gallop, Jane. "Beyond the Phallus." In *Thinking Through the Body*. New York: Columbia University Press, 1988.

Gardner, Paul. *Louise Bourgeois*. New York: Universe Books, 1993.

Gillespie, William H. "A Contribution to the Study of Fetishism," *International Journal of Psychoanalysis* 21 (1940): 401-15.

—. "The Psycho-analytic Theory of Sexual Deviation with Special Reference to Fetishism." In I. Rosen, ed., *The Pathology and Treatment of Sexual Deviation: A Methodological Approach*. 123-45. New York: Oxford, 1964.

Goux, Jean-Joseph. *Oedipus Philosopher*, trans. Catherine Porter. Stanford: Stanford University Press, 1994.

Greenacre, Phyllis. "Certain Relationships between Fetishism and Faulty Development of the Body Image," *Psychoanalytic Study of the Child* 8 (1953), 79-98.

—. "The Fetish and the Transitional Object," *Psychoanalytic Study of the Child* 24 (1969), 144-64.

—. "Fetishism." In *Sexual Deviations*, ed. Ismond Rosen, 79-108. London: Oxford University Press, 1979.

Hegel, G. W. F. *Lectures on the Philosophy of Religion*. 1832. 3 vols, trans. Rev. E. B. Speirs and J. Burdon Sanderson. New York : Humanities Press, 1974.

—. *Philosophy of Mind*, trans. A.V. Miller. Oxford: Clarendon Press, 1971.

Heidegger, Martin. "The Thing." In *Poetry, Language, Thought*, trans. A. Hofstadter, 167-79. New York: Harper and Row, 1971.

Iacono, Alfonzo M. *Le Fétichisme, Histoire d'un concept*. Paris: Presses Universitaires de France, 1992.

Kant, Immanuel. *Zum ewigen Frieden*. In *Werkausgabe Band XI*, herausgegeben von Wilhelm Weischedel, Frankfurt amMain: Suhrkamp, 1977, 195-254.

Keenan, Thomas. "The Point is to (Ex)Change it." In *Fetishism as Cultural Discourse*, ed. Emily Apter and William Pietz, 152-85. Ithica: Cornell University Press, 1993

Kelly, Mary. *Post-Partum Document*. London: Routledge and Kegan Paul, 1983.

Klein, Melanie. "Early Stages of the Oedipus Conflict," (1928). In *The Selected Melanie Klein*, ed. Juliet Mitchell. New York: Free Press, 1986.

—. "The Psychological Principles of Infant Analysis" (1926). In *The Selected Melanie Klein*.

Krips, Henry. *Fetishism: An Erotics of Culture*. Ithica: Cornell University Press, 1999.

Latour, Bruno. *Petite réflexion sur le culte moderne des dieux faitiches*. Le Plessis-Robinson: Synthélabo (Collection: Les Empêcheurs de penser en rond), 1996.

Leiris, Michel. "Alberto Giacometti," *Documents* vol. 1, no. 4 (1929).

L[evy], P[esella]. exhibition review, Peridot Gallery, *Art Digest*, vol. 25 (1 October 1950).

Lippard, Lucy. "Louise Bourgeois: From the Inside Out." In *From the Center: Feminist Essays on Women's Art*. New York: E.P. Dutton & Co., 1976.

Mannoni, Octave. "Je sais bien, mais quand même..." In *Clefs pour l'imaginaire*, 9-33. Paris: Seuil, 1967.

Matlock, Jann. "Masquerading Women, Pathologized Men: Cross-Dressing, Fetishism, and the Theory of Perversion, 1882-1935." In *Fetishism as Cultural Discourse*, ed. Emily Apter and William Pietz, 31-61. Ithica: Cornell University Press, 1993, 31-61.

Mauss, Marcel. *Œuvres*, vol.2 : *Représentations collectives et diversité des civilisations*, ed. Victor Karady. Paris: Éditions de Minuit, 1968.

Mitchell, Juliet. *Mad Men and Medusas: Reclaiming Hysteria and the Effects of Sibling Relations on the Human Condition*. London: Penguin, 2000.

Moyaert, Paul. *Begeren en vereren : Idealisering en sublimering*. Nijmegen: SUN, 2002.

—. "The Sense of Symbols as the Core of Religion." In J. Faulconer, ed., *Transcendence in Philosophy and Religion*, 53-69. Bloomington: Indiana University Press, 2003.

—. "Sur la sublimation chez Lacan." In *La pensée de Jacques Lacan: Questions historiques-problèmes théoriques*, ed. P. Moyaert and S. Lofts, 125-46. Leuven-Paris: Editions Peeters, 1994, Collection "Bibliothèque philosophique de Louvain", vol. 39.

Nixon, Mignon. "Bad Enough Mother," *October* 71 (Winter 1995), 71-92.

—. "'Fantastic Reality': A Note on Louise Bourgeois's *Portrait of C.Y.*," *Sculpture Journal* vol. 5 (2001).

—. "Pretty as a Picture: Louise Bourgeois's *Fillette*," *Parkett* 27 (1991).

Payne, Sylvia. "Some Observations on the Ego Development of the Fetishist," *International Journal of Psychoanalysis* 20 (1939).

Pietz, William. "Fetishism and Materialism: The Limits of Theory in Marx." In *Fetishism as Cultural Discourse*, ed. Emily Apter and William Pietz, 119-51. Ithica: Cornell University Press, 1993.

—. "The Problem of the Fetish," *Res* 9 (Autumn 1985), 5-17.

—. "The Problem of the Fetish, II: The Origin of the Fetish." *Res* 13 (Spring 1987), 23-45.

—. "The Problem of the Fetish, IIIa: Bosman's Guinea and the enlightenment theory of fetishism." *Res* 16 (Autumn 1988), 105-23.

Pouillon, Jean. "Fétiches sans fétichisme." In *Objets du fétichisme*, 135-48.Paris: Nouvelle Revue de Psychanalyse, Numéro 2 (automne 1970).

Rey-Flaud, Henry. *Comment Freud inventa le féthichisme... et réinventa la psychanalyse*. Paris: Èditions Payot et Rivages, 1994.

Ricoeur, Paul. *De l'interprétation. Essai sur Freud*. Paris: Seuil, 1965.

Rose, Barbara. "Race, Sex, and Louise Bourgeois," *Vogue*, September 1987.

Rubin, William S. *Dada, Surrealism, and Their Heritage*. New York: Museum of Modern Art, 1968.

Storr, Robert.interview, *Galeries Magazine*. Paris, (June-July 1990).

Strick, Jeremy. *Louise Bourgeois: The Personages*. St. Louis: Saint Louis Art Museum, 1994.

Suleiman, Susan Rubin. "Playing and Motherhood; or, How to Get the Most out of the Avant-   Garde." In *Representations of Motherhood*, ed. Donna Bassin, Margaret Honey, and Meryle Mahrer Kaplan. New Haven: Yale University Press, 1994.

Taylor, Mark C. *Altarity*. Chicago: The University of Chicago Press, 1987.

Treat, Carolyn. "Louise Bourgeois: Art Is a Guarantee for Sanity," interview, *Kunst & Museum Journal*, vol. 2, no. 6 (1991).

Winnicott, D. W. "Transitional Objects and Transitional Phenomena," *International Journal of Psychoanalysis*, 34, (1953) 88-97.

Wye, Deborah. "A Drama of the Self: Louise Bourgeois as Printmaker," in Wye and Carol Smith, *The Prints of Louise Bourgeois*. New York: Museum of Modern Art, 1994.

—. *Louise Bourgeois*. New York: Museum of Modern Art, 1982.

AUTHOR NOTES

Egidius Berns is professor of Social Philosophy and Social Ethics at the Faculty of Philosophy, Universiteit van Tilburg (Holland). From 1995 to 2001 he was the Director of Foreign Research at the Collège international de Philosophie (Paris). He is the author of *Kringloop en Woekering. Een deconstructieve filosofie van de economie,* (Amsterdam: Boom, 1998), and has written numerous articles on the philosophy of the economy, ethics and Derrida.

Andreas De Block studied philosophy and psychology in Leuven and Gent. He is currently a post-doctoral researcher for the Dutch Council for Scientific Research (NWO) at the University of Nijmegen (Holland), where he is investigating the philosophical implications of Darwinian psychiatry. He is a founding member of the Center for Psychoanalysis and Philosophical Anthropology and the Interdisciplinary Center for the study of Evolution and Behavior. His publications include: *Vragen aan Freud: psychoanalyse en de menselijke natuur* (Amsterdam: Boom, 2003) and *De Vogel van Leonardo: Freuds opvattingen over seksualiteit, cultuur en gezondheid* (Leuven/Leusden: ACCO, 2004).

Christopher Gemerchak is a researcher for the Foundation for Scientific Research (FWO-Vlaanderen) at the Higher Institute of Philosophy of the Katholieke Universiteit Leuven (Belgium). He is the author of *The Sunday of the Negative: Reading Bataille Reading Hegel* (SUNY Press, Series in Hegelian Studies, 2003). He is currently writing a book on fetishism.

Jean-Joseph Goux is professor of French Philosophy at Rice University (Houston, U.S.A.). He has taught at the University of California (San Diego, Berkeley), Duke University and Brown University. He was "Directeur de programme" at the Collège international de Philosophie (Paris) and associate professor at the Ecole des Hautes Etudes en Sciences Sociales. His primary publications include: *Economie et symbolique* (Éd. du Seuil, 1973); *Les iconoclastes* (Éd. du Seuil, 1978), translated together as *Symbolic Economies* (Cornell University Press, 1990); *Les monnayeurs du langage* (Galilée, 1984), translated as *The Coiners of Language* (University of Oklahoma Press, 1994); *Oedipe philosophe* (Aubier, 1990), translated as *Oedipus Philosopher* (Stanford University Press, 1993); and more recently, *Frivolité de la valeur* (Éd. Blusson, 2000).

Paul Moyaert is a Professor of Philosophical Anthropology and Ethics at the Higher Institute of Philosophy of the K.U.Leuven and is a practicing psychoanalyst. His primary publications include: *Begeren en vereren: Idealisering en sublimering* (Nijmegen: SUN, 2002); *De mateloosheid van het christendom: Over naastenliefde, betekenisincarnatie en mystieke liefde* (Nijmegen: SUN, 1998); *Ethiek en sublimatie: over De ethiek van de psychoanalyse van Jacques Lacan* (Nijmegen: SUN, 1994).

Mignon Nixon teaches at the Courtauld Institute of Art, University of London, and is an editor of *October*. She is the author of *'He Disappeared into Complete Silence': Louise Bourgeois and a Psychoanalytic Story of Modern Art* (MIT Press, forthcoming), the editor of *Eva Hesse* (MIT Press, 2002) and the co-editor, with Martha Buskirk, of *The Duchamp Effect* (MIT Press, 1996). Her essays on contemporary art in a psychoanalytic perspective have been published in *October*, the *Oxford Art Journal*, *Divan*, *Parkett*, and *The Sculpture Journal* (UK), as well as in anthologies including *October: The Second Decade, A Companion to Art Theory* (Blackwell, 2002), and the forthcoming *Women Artists at the Millennium* (MIT Press).

FIGURES OF THE UNCONSCIOUS

(Hors série)

- D. DEVREESE, Z. LOTHANE, J. SCHOTTE (éds.), *Schreber revisité*
  1998, 243 p., ISBN 90 6186 908 0, € 30,98

1. PH. VAN HAUTE, J. CORVELEYN (eds.), *Seduction, Suggestion, Psychoanalysis*
   2001, 128 p., ISBN 90 5867 127 5, € 21,07
2. A. DE WAELHENS, W. VER EECKE, *Phenomenology and Lacan on Schizophrenia, after the Decade of the Brain*
   2001, 338 p., ISBN 90 5867 160 7, € 30,98
3. J. CORVELEYN, P. MOYAERT (eds.), *Psychosis: Phenomenological and Psychoanalytical approaches*
   2003, 168 p., ISBN 90 5867 279 4, € 29
4. C.M. GEMERCHAK, *Everyday Extraordinary: Encountering Fetishism with Marx, Freud and Lacan*
   2004, 142 p., ISBN 90 5867 408 8

Drukkerij en Binderij
SCHEERDERS van KERCHOVE
9100 ST.-NIKLAAS